Turning It Around

What needs to be improved at your school? In this essential new book, Todd Whitaker and Courtney Monterecy provide a clear roadmap to making the changes that will bring lasting benefits to your students and staff, whether those changes are small tweaks or larger overhauls.

You'll learn step-by-step ways to diagnose the issues and listen to your staff about what needs to change, to hire more effectively and improve the teachers you have, to implement structures and coaching to address student behavior, and to communicate before you need to. Whitaker and Monterecy also show you how to grow as a leader by making time for what only you can do, by developing other leaders within the building, and by always communicating your why. Each chapter is filled with helpful strategies and inspiring true stories.

With this book's wisdom and practical takeaways, you will have the courage and know-how to implement the important changes your students truly deserve.

Todd Whitaker (@toddwhitaker) is a leading presenter in the field of education, and has written 65 books, including the bestseller *What Great Teachers Do Differently*. He is a former teacher, coach, principal, and professor of educational leadership.

Courtney Monterecy is the principal of Mary E. Fogarty Elementary School in Providence, Rhode Island. In 2020, she was named the Rhode Island Elementary School Principal of the Year, and she is a National Distinguished Principal.

T0384837

Also Available from Routledge Eye on Education

(www.routledge.com/k-12)

What Great Teachers Do Differently: Nineteen Things That Matter Most
Todd Whitaker

What Great Principals Do Differently: Twenty Things That Matter Most
Todd Whitaker

How to Get All Teachers to Become Like Your Best Teachers
Todd Whitaker

Your First Year: How to Survive and Thrive as a New Teacher
Todd Whitaker, Katherine Whitaker, Madeline Whitaker Good

Classroom Management from the Ground Up
Todd Whitaker, Katherine Whitaker, Madeline Whitaker Good

Dealing with Difficult Parents
Todd Whitaker and Douglas Fiore

Dealing with Difficult Teachers
Todd Whitaker

A School Leader's Guide to Dealing with Difficult Parents
Todd Whitaker and Douglas Fiore

Invest in Your Best: 9 Strategies to Grow, Support, and Celebrate Your Most Valuable Teachers
Todd Whitaker, Connie Hamilton, Joseph Jones, T. J. Vari

Turning It Around

Small Steps or Sweeping Changes to Create the School Your Students Deserve

Todd Whitaker and Courtney Monterecy

Routledge
Taylor & Francis Group

NEW YORK AND LONDON

Designed cover image: © Getty Images

First published 2025
by Routledge
605 Third Avenue, New York, NY 10158

and by Routledge
4 Park Square, Milton Park, Abingdon, Oxon, OX14 4RN

Routledge is an imprint of the Taylor & Francis Group, an informa business

© 2025 Todd Whitaker and Courtney Monterecy

The right of Todd Whitaker and Courtney Monterecy to be identified as authors of this work has been asserted in accordance with sections 77 and 78 of the Copyright, Designs and Patents Act 1988.

Library of Congress Cataloging-in-Publication Data
Names: Whitaker, Todd, 1959– author. | Monterecy, Courtney, author.
Title: Turning it around : small steps or sweeping changes to create the school
    your students deserve / Todd Whitaker and Courtney Monterecy.
Description: New York, NY : Routledge, 2024. | Includes bibliographical
    references.
Identifiers: LCCN 2024014265 (print) | LCCN 2024014266 (ebook) |
    ISBN 9781032342795 (hardback) | ISBN 9781032329703 (paperback) |
    ISBN 9781003321323 (ebook)
Subjects: LCSH: School improvement programs. | Educational change. |
    School management and organization.
Classification: LCC LB2822.8 .W554 2024 (print) | LCC LB2822.8 (ebook) |
    DDC 371.2/07—dc23/eng/20240608
LC record available at https://lccn.loc.gov/2024014265
LC ebook record available at https://lccn.loc.gov/2024014266

ISBN: 978-1-032-34279-5 (hbk)
ISBN: 978-1-032-32970-3 (pbk)
ISBN: 978-1-003-32132-3 (ebk)

DOI: 10.4324/9781003321323

Typeset in Palatino
by Apex CoVantage, LLC

Contents

Acknowledgements

From Todd Whitaker:

We would like to thank publisher Lauren Davis for her work on this book. Lauren is truly the best in the business, and her efforts on this were far beyond anything we have experienced in the publication process of a book. She is truly incredible and a gift to education and to authors everywhere. Thank you, Lauren. It was an honor to work with you.

From Courtney Monterecy:

Dedicated to my mom, Linda, my first teacher. Thank you for always setting such a beautiful example in everything you do.

And this book would not be possible without the stories gathered from ten years working with such a special school community. Thank you to every teacher and staff member at Fogarty for making our school the special place it is. What a journey and experience it has been for us all. Through the ups, downs, highs, and lows. Thank you for letting me tell our story and for being an inspiration to so many.

Meet the Authors

Dr. Todd Whitaker has been fortunate to be able to blend his passion with his career. Todd is recognized as a leading presenter in the field of education, and his message about the importance of teaching has resonated with hundreds of thousands of educators around the world. He is a professor of educational leadership at the University of Missouri, and he has spent his life pursuing his love of education by researching and studying effective teachers and principals.

Prior to moving into higher education, he was a mathematics teacher and basketball coach in Missouri. Todd then served as a principal at the middle school, junior high, and high school levels. He was also a middle school coordinator in charge of staffing, curriculum, and technology for the opening of new middle schools.

One of the nation's leading authorities on staff motivation, teacher leadership, and principal effectiveness, Todd has written 65 books, including the national bestseller, *What Great Teachers Do Differently*. Other titles include: *Shifting the Monkey, Dealing with Difficult Teachers, The 10 Minute Inservice, The Ball, What Great Principals Do Differently, Motivating & Inspiring Teachers,* and *Dealing with Difficult Parents*.

Todd is married to Beth, also a former teacher and principal, who is the coordinator of the Educational Leadership program at the University of Missouri. They are the parents of three children: Katherine, Madeline, and Harrison.

Courtney Monterecy is the principal of Mary E. Fogarty Elementary School in Providence, Rhode Island. Prior to being a principal, she served the students of Providence for over two decades: as an ESL classroom teacher, a Reading Coach, an elementary school ELL Specialist, and an Assistant Principal.

Throughout her ten years as principal at Fogarty, she has been recognized for her efforts in school turnaround. In 2020 she was named the Rhode Island Elementary School Principal of the Year, and is a National Distinguished Principal.

Courtney has spent her years at Fogarty working to create a school culture and climate that children, staff, and families want to be a part of. She believes that in the stressful changing times in education, it's important to keep joy and fun at the forefront, emphasizing and prioritizing unique events and initiatives, such as Ice Skating Club, 80s Day, Zumba Parent Committee meetings, and Coffee by the Curb.

She has coached and partnered with three Assistant Principals who have gone on to successfully lead their own schools, and continues to coach, mentor, and support aspiring and early career principals. She has presented sessions such as *Transformation at the Elementary Level: Culture and Climate,* and *Having Difficult Conversations While Continuing to Support School Culture* at the Rhode Island Association of School Principals' annual summer conference.

One of Courtney's proudest moments was when the *Boston Globe* wrote an article about Fogarty's impressive turnaround and high marks on culture and climate among students, staff, and families, titled: "This School Is the Best Kept Secret in Providence."

Courtney lives in Cranston, Rhode Island, with her husband Jason.

Introduction

The Journey

We are so proud to share *Turning It Around* with you. If you are reading this, you are probably working to find ways to improve your school to better serve your students. That is fantastic, and we are happy to support you in any role that can inspire and facilitate that process. We thought that sharing a little bit of the journey in developing and writing this book might provide some insight to the reader.

Many years ago, Todd had the good fortune of becoming principal of a school that was not in a very positive state; morale was low, student achievement was stagnant, behavior of faculty and students was very non-productive and at times, it was actually destructive. The reputation of the school was not stellar, to say the least. Teachers did not want to join the faculty, and the best teachers were looking to depart. The journey to transfer away from this type of environment and convert the school to a place of pride that worked to meet the needs of all students was challenging but incredibly gratifying.

This journey became the impetus to writing a book. It was tentatively titled *Turning It Around* but was not written. Instead, pieces of this journey became their own books—*Dealing with Difficult Teachers, Dealing with Difficult Parents (And with Parents in Difficult Situations), Motivating and Inspiring Teachers, Leading School Change*, and so on—which described and hopefully

DOI: 10.4324/9781003321323-1

provided educators a pathway to enhance parts of their schools and districts. Additionally, several books were coauthored with school culture guru Steve Gruenert about school culture itself—*School Culture Rewired* and *Leveraging the Impact of Culture and Climate*, to name two—to help school leaders build a more positive school climate and enhance their organizational culture. Books were written for teachers (*What Great Teachers Do Differently*) and principals (*What Great Principals Do Differently*) that are also guidebooks to school improvement.

The desire to write a book about and titled *Turning It Around* was always swirling around for Todd as he thought it was a much-needed piece for educators everywhere. The idea crystallized when he had a chance to meet Courtney after he was invited to work with her school in Providence, Rhode Island. Wow! Her school was indeed a "Turn Around" school. She and the dynamic faculty she put together have made a struggling high needs school into a sanctuary in the city. Part of their journey was guided and inspired by some of Todd's writings, but mostly it was led by her dedication, vision, brilliance, and hard work. When we met and shared our journeys we realized that now was the time, and Courtney was the person to do this project with.

The Book

Though this book was inspired by the dramatic growth and success of a couple of schools, it is really written and designed to help any school or school district "turn around." We have attempted to provide steps to advance any pathway in the school. Whether it is increasing staff morale or school climate, improving student behavior, building family and community support, dealing with negative staff members, enhancing the culture, or even deciding the best place to start in your own setting, this book is designed to help with school wide change or any smaller aspects that your school needs.

Hopefully the book tells a story that you can understand from beginning to end; we also want it to be a reference and support guide that you can use on as "as needed" approach. For example, if you just want to focus on reducing resistance to improvement, you can start there and apply that to your setting. There may be pieces of your school that you rightfully have great pride in, and you have no interest in "turning them around" or even gently tweaking them. That is wonderful. We want you to use that as a point of pride. There is no need to change everything when you really just need to alter certain things. So, we hope the format of this books helps in the specific areas you desire.

However, we also realize that similar to sprucing up a home, when you paint the kitchen walls it may make the cabinets look shabby. And replacing the cabinets may cause you to reflect on the badly scarred flooring situation. But we hope as your school moves forward, you can celebrate each of the steps and improvements you have made. Always remember, education is the improvement business rather than the perfection business.

The one thing we do not want *Turning It Around* to be is an indictment or acknowledgement of current failure. People who read self-help books rarely need to do so, but many people who scoff at them could benefit. One of our favorite sayings is: "Most people who have imposter syndrome probably shouldn't, but many people who do not have imposter syndrome probably should."

We hope that this book provides some direction for you on your journey and also some reinforcement that you are doing the right thing. Remember, change is inevitable, growth is optional. If you are reading this book, then your school and your students are fortunate that you care and are working to make a difference. Though a core of this book is about a story with one school, the real purpose is to help anyone see how parts of the journey of one school can help develop an understanding and provide a path for any school and in particular—your school. Whether the examples are elementary or secondary, we have great faith that our readers can envision the underlying message and see how it applies in their setting. We are so proud of school leaders, and we know that Turing It Around can only result from the caring and dedicated leadership that your school has. Go get 'em!

Turning It Around is not about where we are or where we have been; it is all about where we are going. We hope this book supports you on your journey. We are honored you have chosen to let us be a partner on your path of improvement. Let's get this party started.

I

Determining Where to Begin

I

Determining Where to Begin

1

Learning from Those Around You

There is a quote that hangs on my office wall that says: "You weren't hired to maintain the status quo. You were hired to make a difference and make an impact. Don't ever forget this." When I first saw this quote (via a tweet from @JustinTarte), it resonated with me. It reminds me and inspires me to never give up, to never fall into a culture of compliance and settling for *maintaining*. I have chosen to be the principal of *this* school and worked hard to have the privilege of calling myself that. If I don't begin the improvement process, who is going to? As I took on the challenge of leading the lowest performing elementary school in my state, I felt a little overwhelmed. Not only was the school in poor academic standing; it was also in need of drastic change in other areas as well: the physical plant, staff culture and climate, parent involvement, student safety, systems, student behavior, adult behavior, routines . . . in short, everything. When our goal is to change one thing—for example, test scores—it quickly becomes obvious that to do this task we have to align many things which can support, or at least allow, any positive change to occur.

These words may also resonate with school leaders who are at more successful schools with a less crucial need to make dramatic changes, yet there are smaller areas that may prevent their schools from reaching their full potential. There might be things that gnaw at your subconscious that you know should be better for staff and/or students. Does anyone take on a leadership

DOI: 10.4324/9781003321323-3

position with no desire to change or improve the school; isn't the core of school leadership about making things better for students? And for the adults as well? Maintaining the status quo means no forward movement and no growth. It means that the good things have already reached the ceiling of their climb, and that we are accepting and tolerating things we know should be better. So, wherever you are in your journey to turn things around at your school, the key is knowing exactly where you are, *why* you are there, and where you'd like to be.

Own the Situation

No one prepares you for starting in the summer, as a brand new principal, and the first time you walk into your office. This experience can vary based on your previous connections (or lack thereof) with a district or a school. I visualized a scenario where a district higher-up would greet me at the door, hand me the keys—literally and figuratively—and show me around. In reality, I arrived early on the morning of July 1st, walked up to the front door, and realized I had no way of getting inside. A custodian let me in. I entered my office and was shocked and overwhelmed by the state of the tiny room: there were about ten cases of copy paper piled up in the corner by the window. There was a small wooden desk in another corner, covered with a Dollar Tree pink and white plastic polka dot tablecloth. The previous administrator—an Acting Principal—had left me a few items that I still cannot "connect the dots" as to 1) why these items made the cut to be left for me, and 2) how the items would support or be meaningful to this school. One item was a gift certificate from a local hardware store, saying "one free rental—popcorn machine." No context, no note from the administrator, just the certificate. Another item was a large sheet of chart paper with barely-legible scrawl of what looked to be a list of things that the previous leadership may have been working on. Just words, however; no next steps or information. The third thing that was left on the tiny wooden desk was a black plastic magazine file with a copy of the teachers' union contract and some blank checks to the school bank account. I felt a pang of panic: *Do I need to go to the bank? How do I even get access to our bank account?* But much more immediate questions remained: Would I get a key to the building? Will I get a security code? Where were the keys to everybody's classrooms, offices, closets, kitchen, etc.?

This school was officially the lowest achieving school in my state, with a revolving door of administrators and a recent mass exodus of teachers. I was left with a staff composed of several pre-existing personnel files, displaced teachers who'd lost their joy of teaching, and veteran teachers who were "sticking it out" in poor teaching conditions, but with extremely low morale and resentment toward the school district-level leadership for what they perceived to be allowing their school to sink so low. Parent engagement was almost non-existent, the building was filthy . . . popcorn machine?! It would be funny if it weren't so bleak. Was the prior administration sitting back with popcorn, so to speak, watching the tragic decline of the school unfold?

In some ways, starting completely from scratch, with nothing, can be beneficial. This way, you have no choice but to *own everything*. Owning everything is overwhelming and time consuming, but when working to turn a school around, the hard truth is that you're going to be putting some (probably a lot of) extra time in, especially at first. Your goal is to put in place structures and routines that are so clear that eventually you *can* hand them over to others within your building. You cannot be the only person managing everything; you need to own everything for others to be able to join in on the process. You can take ownership of the school's data, the school's safety and operational procedures, the school's staffing, the organization and structure of the front office. Bit by bit, your style and your design will be incorporated into already-existing protocols, or will be the driving force behind new, much-needed protocols.

Listen to Your Staff About What Needs to Change

So, what specifically are you owning? What areas need turning around at your school? Some of you may be leading schools in which you were already a member of the staff, either as a teacher, support staff, or Assistant Principal. Some of you may be leading schools that you had never stepped foot in until the day you were appointed, and some of you may be preparing to lead schools in cities you plan to relocate to, having almost no prior knowledge of the state of affairs inside that school's walls.

No matter how intimate your knowledge of a school is, it's important to start with knowing *why* certain things need turning around. Ask, *How did this get to be the way it is today?* Knowing the why—the root cause—will help you make lasting change rather than slapping a temporary Band-Aid on existing problems. This background knowledge can also help us understand which things are sacred cows and are going to be the most challenging to change, and which may have fewer fans and thus be much easier to alter.

Start by establishing honest, two-way communication with "your people." It is your school community—your staff, your community partners, your families—who can give you the most valuable insight as to why you are where you are. Listen to your stakeholders. In my two decades as an educator, I've witnessed leaders coming into a school or district and looking at achievement data alone to determine a path toward turnaround. That hardly ever works, at least not toward lasting change. Low achievement data does not mean that a renewed focus on instructional learning objectives is the right, or only, path to bettering a school. Much like with any problem or issue in life, we need to treat the root cause, not just the symptom. Is low student achievement data the *only* area for improvement in an otherwise idyllic school? In that case, maybe a renewed focus on instructional objectives and learning targets is truly a great next step toward improvement. Many times, however, low student achievement data is one symptom of a larger problem and comes in tandem with other concerns: high teacher turnover, poor culture and climate, lack of professional development and growth opportunities for staff, low parent and community involvement, unsafe or unappealing physical building conditions. Without knowing the root cause, it is much more challenging to find the root solution.

If you are a newer administrator, it's especially important to listen, so the staff does not view you as "just another person who was sent to fix their school." It really is *their* school. Some of your staff may have spent a couple decades in this building that you are walking into. During that time, they've made lifelong memories and have gone through significant experiences. You want to be sure the teachers in this school share your vision, or at the very least agree with the need for change. Your staff must be part of the process. It has to be an "all hands-on deck" approach, where every member of the staff is aware of 1) where you are, 2) where you need to go, and 3) how you can get there. Even better if every member of the staff feels truly invested in the process.

Here are some ways to establish communication to listen, diagnose what's really going on, and determine where you need to go.

1. Schedule Regular Meetings with *All* Staff Groups

One method is to schedule regular meeting times with all of your staff groups to elicit feedback and suggestions for improvement. Sometimes we take for granted the built-in times each week to meet with grade level or content teams of classroom teachers. But you might not have existing time set aside to meet with all subgroups of your staff: your Teacher Assistants, Specialist team, or Clerical staff. Memos are great, but face time is invaluable. When you meet with a specific group of professionals, you can start by asking what they need from you.

◆ Teacher Assistants: Teacher Assistants are oftentimes the unsung heroes of your school. These professionals can either partner with our teachers and create a co-teaching environment or be grossly under-utilized; it's up to us to ensure that we are maximizing their potential. TAs work closely with our youngest and most in-need learners in classrooms across the school. They see it all: if they wanted to, they could tell you things you never knew were happening in classrooms, in hallways, and amongst staff. TAs are so valuable to the smooth functioning of a school day: they are responsible for supporting students during specialist periods, during lunch, and in the Bus Room. In many ways, I felt I was bonding with this team more than any other team in the early years, since they are such integral parts of the common areas and would be such big parts of the redesign of so many of our procedures and routines. Often times some of your Teacher Assistants may have a long history in the school and can provide insights into how we got to where we are now. Meeting with this group of professionals kept me close to their daily efforts and created an open line of communication for them to come to me with any concerns or feedback. It also equipped me with more insight and strategic planning for when I met with classroom teachers. When examining data with the kindergarten team, for example, I was able to support teachers in creating intervention plans that included utilizing TAs rather than keeping them isolated in the back corner of a room. We had this amazing opportunity for students to get additional, intensified one-on-one time with a professional—why is she stapling papers in the corner?

◆ Specialist Teams: The Specialist team can make or break a school and is one of the most crucial groups of teachers to empower. A classroom teacher or content area teacher has a student in front of them every single day for a whole school year. Specialists, though, have the opportunity to affect students' lives for multiple years. At the elementary level, specialists are often in art, music, physical education, etc. At the secondary level, it can be the same teachers as well as teachers who are involved in foreign language, family and consumer science, technology, etc. Many times they are the only person in this role and connect with students in a different way than a core teacher. Plus, they often have school-wide vision and connections others may lack. They have essential value but may at times feel like they are on the fringe of the school community.

In a K–5 elementary school, a Music teacher can influence a child's life for six consecutive years—talk about wanting the right people on that team! Specialists, like TAs, see everything. They know which classrooms are having a tough day, they know which students seem to be "off," and they are in all the common areas throughout the day. I leaned on this team very much as we restructured the way we managed the cafeteria, the Bus Room, and hallway passage in between classes. A Specialist teacher affects students and families for multiple years and has the opportunity to be one of the most constant sources of encouragement and motivation in a child's life. I instituted a weekly meeting with my Specialist Team in Year One and used that time to touch base on what materials they may need, planning special events, debriefing and reflecting on common areas, and sharing student successes and challenges. Each week, I'd ask the Specialist Team if there were any students whose behaviors seem to be on the rise. Thinking of students that are struggling academically or behaviorally, the hope was to "catch" something that may be happening before it's gone too far. This team has been incredibly valuable in reporting concerning behaviors, offering supports to our students, and following up to offer supports to our teachers. I consider this weekly check-in critical to staying on top of student behaviors and classroom management.

These meetings can also be opportunities for the principal and any others who are part of the conversation to learn about things so that they can trumpet these efforts on a wider school-wide or even district-wide level. Once we start having more frequent and regular open discussions about building needs (materials, staffing), student behavior concerns (which students are on behavior plans or have 504 plans that this team must also adhere to), and other topics that these teachers would not normally be privy to, educators may start to see the school with a stronger sense of ownership as well as a broader vision of what school is and can be. This pays off in how they view the work; they are invested in the bigger picture.

Adopting a Class

Here is an example of a way Specialist team members grew to become significant informal leaders in a school. We had each Specialist teacher (i.e., music, art, physical education, etc.) "adopt" grade levels or "adopt" classrooms in need. Let's say a 5th-grade classroom was without a permanent teacher (staffing shortages are the new normal, unfortunately). One of the Specialist teachers "adopted" that classroom. If one of the teachers through a scheduling fluke has a few periods each week that they are unassigned, and rather than seeing that as personal time, they report directly to that classroom to be a consistent support as the class adjusts to having a revolving door of substitute teachers. The benefit of this scenario is that students get this additional support from an adult who has possibly known them for several years. It works well at the upper levels too—the high school art teacher may have a student for multiple years, whereas a math teacher may only teach sophomores. This strategy is also infusing and demonstrating a "team player" mentality being lived out in real time. A particular teacher thought of this idea on their own, and it has now improved the culture of the Specialist team. This type of innovative and inspirational growth may start with one person on one day, but the big picture thinking and the selfless efforts are essential to long-term growth in a school. This type of "all hands on deck" attitude is not born overnight and is definitely not the result of specific directives. However, the idea may be a direct result of getting face time with me each week, even if it is a brief 15 to 30 minutes. The meetings bring this particular team "in."

◆ Clerical Staff: The front office represents the tone of the school to outsiders and insiders. Calm is good and disarray is stressful in a school setting. School front office staff have the most unique position in the school. They see absolutely everything that goes on in your school, with the exception of the daily teaching and learning that occurs in classrooms. When people think of a school, or think of the education profession, the image that is conjured up in most people's minds is that of classroom instruction: teaching and learning. Yet these clerical professionals are running on full bore energy, busier than many people could imagine, handling the hundreds of *other* aspects of running a school. Because, as we all know, if the fort isn't held down, then the principal's day becomes consumed with reacting, responding, and cleaning up messes, rather than allowing building leaders the time to support coaching, developing, and instruction. Front office staff can make or break the smooth functioning of all protocols, processes, and operational tasks. They needed to be on the team, and fast. With front office staff, I learned that asking "What do you need from *me*?" works a lot better than "Here's what I need you to do." Of course, the things we needed our clerks to do were embedded in the conversations. But never as the lead. What do you need from me, *so that you can safely and securely dismiss students?* What do you need from me, *so that you can enter all budget requisitions in a timely manner?*

Meeting with your people sends the message that each subgroup is important to you. I learned how critical it is to stop and thank these groups of people often and recognize the important work that they do—so easy to neglect when running a busy building. When people feel valued, they want to continue to do the good work that got them praise in the first place.

Hitting the Reset Button with Clerical Staff

I realized at the end of each busy, hectic day that my clerks and I had become like ships passing in the night. Glenda would leave messages taped to my door or written on sticky notes placed on my keyboard . . . her intention was so that I would not miss the message, but what was happening was a pile-up of random slips of paper everywhere we looked. Too much room for error and confusion. Isabelle would be buzzing visitors in all day and casually mention to me after 4:00 pm that the Department of Youth,

Children, and Families had stopped in to meet with a student. I'd be stunned that no one thought to tell me . . . too much possibility for a missed opportunity to support students and families. I realized this was learned behavior during years of chaos—we needed to hit the reset button.

There is never a good time to pull your entire clerical staff from the Main Office at the same time; who's manning the ship if everyone is at a meeting? My Assistant Principal and I decided to schedule a meeting after school twice per month, for the last 20 minutes before the clerks were scheduled to go home. It was a risky move since we often had late students and needed to remain in the Main Office, but whenever it worked out, we grabbed the time. We started each meeting by asking for ways that *we* could support *them*. This was eye-opening, as Glenda and Isabelle would share things that teachers were requesting that were stressing them out, or how the smallest interruptions would affect smooth operations in the office. One thing that we learned was how stressed our clerks were during the morning rush: that 15–20 minutes immediately after the bell where late students were buzzing the front door, parents were still buzzing to come in, hoping to speak to clerks about bus passes or changes to emergency forms. So when school staff came into the office and unintentionally added to that busy rush. ("Good morning Isabelle, can you pull these three permanent record folders for me?" "Hi Grace, can you call Wilber's mom? She only speaks Spanish. Can you let her know he forgot his clarinet today and he has Band practice at 10:30." "Isabelle, can I fax something? How do you fax again?") Same thing with the last 20 to 30 minutes of the day—the office is inundated with early dismissals, phone calls from parents or day care providers, and other end-of-day deadlines. We immediately came up with a new policy to support our clerks: If you have a need in the front office, and if it is not a time-sensitive emergency, please refrain from coming into the office during the first half hour or last half hour of the day. That quickly alleviated the overcrowded feeling in the office during critical times such as arrival and dismissal. Grace and Isabelle could devote all of their attention to safe and orderly operations. Additionally, we came up with a protocol for any sort of clerical request, such as pulling permanent record folders or printing out emergency information. Staff were to email the requests to Isabelle and/or Grace, copying me, with the title of the email to read: Clerical Request. This served two purposes: it eliminated the pop-ins and the hastily scribbled sticky notes that Isabelle and Grace would write to remind themselves to do that clerical task, and it also allowed me to follow up with our clerks if clerical requests started to pile up.

Grace would often fall behind in entering budget requisitions, which would result in our school not receiving stock room items or other budgetary needs in a timely manner. I initially attributed it to her having a lack of urgency to complete these tasks. When I asked her *what she needed from me* to meet deadlines, her answer surprised me: I need a quiet place to work.

You may chuckle at that—*good luck finding a peaceful quiet corner in an elementary school main office, Grace!* But she was absolutely right: her desk was positioned at the main in-house phone switchboard. Each time a classroom teacher called the office, she had to stop whatever she was doing and attend to the phone call. If the call was to request assistance with a behavior concern, she'd also then need to get on the walkie and radio for help. She felt that she had so many interruptions, she'd lose her focus and put things on the back burner that she had initially been working on. We eventually came up with a plan that when Grace had pressing high-importance tasks to complete, Isabelle would cover the office for an hour, while Grace would work in my office and close the door. Her productivity with tasks that required attention to detail skyrocketed when we started doing that.

Meeting with your TAs, Specialists, and Clerical Staff will help you uncover how your school really needs to improve, and it will help you make everyone feel like part of the improvement process.

But how can you get the most out of those meetings? Remember that the goal is to ask questions. No one wants to meet with their principal, their boss, and be talked at for 45 minutes. People want to feel heard, valued, and appreciated. By asking questions, we are able to ascertain how the members of each team understand their daily responsibilities and what they experience each day.

A few questions that have worked for me, that you can try with your teams and subgroups:

- ◆ What do you need from me, in order to. . . . (fill in the blank)?
- ◆ What is the barrier, keeping you from. . . . (fill in the blank)?
- ◆ How do you see yourself being most helpful during your admin periods? (to Specialists)

Telling your teams WHY they are so important to you, and to the functioning of your building, is always valuable. The more people hear that they are appreciated (and why!), the more likely they are to continue behaving in a way to live up to the praise and expectations.

2. Get Wish Lists from Teachers

Aside from meeting with various subgroups, another way to determine what needs to change at your school is to encourage teachers to submit ideas. Ask them to provide their own wish lists for school improvement. Teachers will want to know the benefits to them, so you may want to start with the angle of WIIFM—What's In It For Me? You can organize before- and after-school meetings where teachers could jot down a "wish list" of supports, materials, programs, or ideas that they think will help improve your school. You can attend these meetings and set the tone by asking, "If you could have anything to help you do your job more effectively, what would it be? Feel free to think outside the box!"

In our case, we then used the wish list for a state grant application, but you could implement this idea even if you're not applying for funding. For our grant, we created large chart paper categories with different, big ideas for the money: After School Programming, In-School Supports, Teacher Capacity-Building, Instructional Programs and Materials, etc. As teachers jotted ideas down on sticky notes and added them to the papers, I encouraged them to keep the great ideas—big or small—coming. My Assistant Principal and I posed questions such as:

"What does your ideal school or classroom look like?" As teachers answered these questions, we'd press them to backwards map on how we could get there. Many teachers suggested "luxuries" such as additional funds to pay teachers to teach an after-school program, or full-time building based substitute teachers whose primary responsibility would be to cover classrooms so that teachers could attend out-of-district PD or observe best practices in a colleague's classroom. Many teachers insightfully requested additional social-emotional supports for students. As teachers' wish lists grew, it became clear that even the most change-resistant teachers could get on board with new materials and new opportunities that would make their jobs more enjoyable or easier.

From these meetings, my leadership team was able to write the grant proposal by connecting and incorporating almost every idea that the teachers had come up with. Were there some items on the lists that were completely unfeasible and almost comical? Sure. Were some suggestions so regressive they were actually offensive, such as the in-house detention room staffed by a retired police officer? Yikes. But people had contributed so many ideas that it was easy to omit some while not losing momentum. The grant included two new partnerships with outside educational agencies: one focused on social-emotional supports, one focused on instructional interventions and building teacher capacity around management of targeted groups. It also included the formation of a Teacher Leadership team, additional supports for our Newcomer ELL students, substantially more professional development on teachers' own time, additional training for staff in new programs, and an intensive after school program for students reading below grade level.

3. Lead Your Staff in Doing an "Initiative Dump"

It can be valuable to stop—wherever you are in your leadership journey—and survey the staff to realize what *they* think the school's priorities are, or what *they* believe to be the top priorities we are tackling as a school. The first thing many administrators may think when reading that sentence is, *Teachers should know exactly what we're focusing on! Every year we review our goals and plans starting from Day One!* Of course as leaders, our goal is to be clear and communicative—we've shared our School Improvement Plan broadly, and the faculty likely either have a copy or had a hand in writing it. Teachers (should) know the goals and strategies that our school is prioritizing and utilizing to measure growth and progress toward academic and social-emotional goals.

But I have learned it isn't always as cut and dry. When staff have been working in a school building for years—a few years or a few decades—there is also something to be said about things lingering, and "taking up space." Which projects, partnerships, and programs are still a priority at your school? *You* may know, but has it been explicitly stated? And honestly sometimes, we as leaders forget things too. It's easy to get swept up in the sea of changes coming at us from central office or the state department of education.

Whether you've been leading your school for ten minutes, ten months, or ten years, it's eye-opening to do an Initiative Dump with your staff at large. Many teachers reported feeling the exercise was "cathartic," similar to cleaning out a closet. I realized that having more ideas and more supports was not necessarily a good thing, and that we needed to calibrate amongst our staff what our SEL playbook would look like (see box on the next page). I asked myself if we had thrown too much out there, or too much at them, fast and furious.

Less is more. When teachers have a clear, regularly-updated list of expectations and initiatives, it supports planning and collaboration. More is not better. My teachers were able to collaborate during the Initiative Dump on how some initiatives were taking too much time away from instruction, or how some programs or tools weren't as culturally responsive as they would like. We were able to narrow our focus to ensure the most important things were being addressed, and we were able to share why we felt this way in our decision-making. Our ultimate goal was greater support for students, increased attention to proactive conflict resolution, and building caring classroom communities. Throwing everything at the wall to see what stuck was jamming our teachers up. Slow and steady wins the race!

For me, the best part was that the teachers felt ownership moving forward from that meeting. They knew why we were doing what we were doing, and it made sense to them. They are the front lines, working with our students every day and addressing the dozens of conflicts—whether tiny or large—that come from the classroom. They should have a voice in choosing what is working and what is going to move our school forward.

SEL Initiative Dump

At my school, we had been working to incorporate additional supports in Social-Emotional Learning (SEL). Over my first few years at the school, we'd brought in a new SEL curriculum, we had announced many school-wide read alouds to incorporate common language into the school, we are a Positive Behavior Interventions and Supports (PBIS) school, and we'd had several district initiatives sent to elementary schools as well. We were currently in the process of getting all teachers trained in Restorative Practices, and the murmurs were starting . . . teachers were starting to feel like there was "too much" happening and weren't sure which initiatives took priority. During a faculty meeting, I led my staff in an "Initiative Dump." We sat in the Library with a blank easel of chart paper, and I asked them to call out any and every SEL initiative they felt was currently happening at our school—whether they were using it or not—and I jotted it down on the chart paper.

Teachers called out answers: *PBIS. Star Bucks* (our individual-student reward system that is part of PBIS). *Restorative Practices. No Bully. How Full Is Your Bucket. Positive Action* (the SEL Curriculum our school had adopted). *PlayWorks Recess. Kindness Ambassadors. Kingian Nonviolence. Building a Beloved Community. Mindfulness and Yoga in the Classroom*, etc., the list continued.

These are all wonderful, quality programs, initiatives, books, or outside agencies that had at one point been a focus at our school. However, there was some overlap in the programs that could confuse or overwhelm even the most informed, organized teachers. For example: the *No Bully* program had mentored our school for a few years, and recommends that if a child is feeling bullied, we assemble a "Solution Team" led by a staff member, including a group of the child's peers, so that the child is able to talk about their feelings, and the team can come up with solutions. However, this overlapped or clashed with some of the philosophies of the other trainings and programs we had, and with some of the district's mandates and policies. Just because a school has done so many wonderful things and has amassed a deep "bag of tricks" to support SEL, doesn't mean that 1) your people are still doing everything as it was rolled out in the past, or 2) it all needs to continue. Often times it ends up that people are only doing the most current thing, as they potentially assumed that everything else was old news.

So after we listed every SEL program, initiative, and tool, we then mapped out which ones we felt were worth moving forward with and which could be put on a shelf. We would continue to be a PBIS school, and hold on to all the tools and strategies that come with that philosophy and training. We scrapped other initiatives, and took certain aspects of many initiatives or programs that we felt were really impactful, to piece together a working, sensible list of expectations and streamline our efforts. We wanted to get the most "bang for our buck" with the numerous tools and supports we'd compiled in a few short years.

Initiative dumps can be a worthwhile way to see whether everyone is truly on the same page about your school's goals. They also help building leaders provide meaningful supports and hold everyone accountable for what *the staff has decided* will be our path forward, and avoids the pockets of staff who may be unintentionally rowing against the tide saying, "I thought we were still doing that."

Set the Tone from Day One

Our jobs have changed and evolved over the years. But one thing that will never change, no matter what standards and curricula come down the pike? Relationships. When we're tasked with turning around a school, we need to prioritize the value of relationships with staff. Listening to different groups, as discussed earlier in the chapter, is one key aspect of relationship-building. But relationship-building is also about setting the tone. And it needs to start on day one, orientation day.

In preparing for the official beginning of our school turn-around journey, I felt the intense pressure to set the right tone. I'd been working all summer, either alone or with small groups of people. I had crafted updated policies and procedures; I had designed schedules, updated school forms that would need to be rolled out . . . I was ready.

But were *they*? I knew that more important than any of these technical things or trainings, I had to get *people on board*. I had to eliminate the mindset of "that's the way we've always done things" and inspire people to want to change the way of doing business as usual. Not an easy task to check off a list:

- ◆ Introduce new recess policy
- ◆ Sign off on bloodborne pathogens video
- ◆ Hand out room keys
- ◆ Change entire staff's mindset and ensure they're on board!

It is not going to happen on Day One—it is going to be some-thing that happens over time, but Orientation Day is critical in setting the tone for the work ahead.

Consider what you want to focus on when you prepare your slide deck, breakout sessions, team-building activities, and other ideas for Orientation Day. I made sure to include what I considered to be inspirational or thought-provoking videos, excerpts, or quotes from educators whose work I thought would be critical in moving our school forward. I included Rita Pierson's TED Talk, "Every kid needs a champion," in which she emphasizes the importance of relationships. Rita embodies the best of all of us; to me, she represents a teacher who dedicated her life to bringing out the best in her students.

I felt that if Rita's TED Talk couldn't bring a shred of hope and inspiration to an educator, it was a bit of a red flag. I was looking forward to using the Talk to veer off into the discussions and sections of the day dedicated to these areas of need. During the video, which is only seven and a half minutes long, I intently studied the faces of my staff as they watched. People's faces were lit up—smiling, nodding, as if they were in the actual audience that day, watching Rita do her thing. At the end as Rita walked off stage and her TED Talk audience clapped, my staff members clapped also. I sighed with relief: the group wasn't so hardened that they were rolling their eyes at her message of hope and inspiration. We can do this. I had the power of the first day of school on my side, that time when even the most negative voices come to the table with a clean slate and the potential for a fresh start.

Keep the Message Going

I love the part of the TED Talk when Rita shares that she would tell her students that the school administration put them all together as a class because they were the best students and she was the best teacher. She told them that they were put together so that they could show the other classes how it's done, especially when walking the halls. She gave her students a motto to recite: "I am somebody, I was somebody when I got here, and I'll be a better somebody when I leave." She says, "If you say it long enough, it starts to be a part of you." I have shamelessly stolen that idea and use it in many classrooms on the first days of school.

As I walk the building on the first day, and over the first few weeks, I visit classrooms and pretend I'm letting the students in on a secret. I say, "Miss Danvers, do you mind if I tell them our secret?" I steal Rita's trick in every classroom and tell them that they can't tell the other classes, but this class was put together specially just to set the example for all the other classes in the school. The teachers are used to this schtick by now and partner with me to get the point across. We want to be the best-behaved class when walking the hallways. We are going to show everyone how to line up in the morning out on the blacktop. When I know that some of my students have heard this in years past, I'll start with "*some* of you were in my special class last year, so you know what I'm talking about."

For the adults, as we've made our major staffing changes and have shown visible improvements in data and school culture, I remain consistent with my messaging that this is the best team and that I would not want to work with any other team. Importantly, this time *it's true*. If I didn't feel that way, I wouldn't say it. I try to be as vocal about how I feel about our team in the hopes of inspiring them to continue fighting hard to turn our school around.

Final Thoughts

Whether we're turning around one specific area of a school—or pretty much everything—it's important to start with owning the situation, taking control of what needs to change, and looking at the root cause. The best way to find out where to begin is to talk to everyone in the school—not just teachers. Meet with all staff groups (including TAs, Specialists, and Clerical Staff), in addition to getting wish lists from teachers and doing an initiative dump. Prioritize relationships and set the tone from day one to get everyone on board—it's their school, and you all have the same ultimate goal of helping kids. You're all in it together!

2

How Does Your Building Look and Feel?

Getting the year off to the right start by listening and developing relationships is key. But the physical aspects of the building matter too. Physical changes may seem peripheral to your work on the core issues. However, making positive, visible, nonthreatening changes can be a quick way to impact the perception of the school. It can make people feel that, "Wow! Things are happening around here. Things are different." In fact, changing a school's physical appearance is one of the few things that can impact all parties. When the entrance hallway and office area become colorful and inviting instead of dark and unappealing, this impacts everyone: staff returning, students entering the school, parents, community members, and even district office people when they venture over. Everyone can get a sense of change and improvement in the school. When things look better, people often feel better. That's why we vacuum when company is coming over. By focusing on the visible environment, we remember that we're converting the school house into a school home.

But where do you begin? Being brand new to your school is actually a fantastic advantage when dealing with the physical environment. If you have been there for several years, it may affect how you "see" your building. We can easily become blind to things that are right before our eyes. You can get used to discolored walls, peeling paint, and unsafe conditions. Walking

DOI: 10.4324/9781003321323-4

into a school with "fresh eyes" can be so valuable: not only when looking at physical areas for improvement—imperfections of the school such as chipping paint or broken floor tiles—but also when looking at layout and use of spaces such as the main office and foyer/hallways.

Capitalize on your "fresh eyes" before you become too familiar and comfortable with the school. As much as we want organization and order, we will eventually sink into the "walk right by something and stop actually *seeing* it" pattern. We might travel past the same metal filing cabinet in the main hallway for about three months before we actually "see" it. With our minds racing with thoughts of student behavior concerns, IEP deadlines, classroom walkthroughs, and fire drills, we can easily lose sight of what the building looks like to someone new. Realize that if you have been in a school for a while, it's worth inviting others over who are not familiar with the building so they can provide a fresh viewpoint for you—particularly if they watch HGTV! Not only will they notice things, but they may also have some ideas that can help. They are not acclimated to the culture yet so they are often better at spotting areas of potential improvement. New people are living the "first impression" and that is an important place to start.

Some schools have closets stuffed with old curricular items, outdated technology, and boxes of books and workbooks that would be much better off in children's hands than sitting in a closet. Some schools have murals on their walls that have faded, or out-of-date signage (imagine walking into a school today and seeing a yellowed sign pointing to the "smoking area"). But people walk by things like this and don't even see them anymore. Fresh eyes are so valuable. To begin, do a facilities walk right away if you're a new administrator. Go with your Facilities Director (which might be a fancy name for your only custodian). You can also invite a colleague (or anyone with a good eye for style) if you'd like. This is a great thing to do when the building is empty of staff and students; it ensures that you're only looking for physical building issues and you won't be distracted by lessons, classroom issues, or student behavior. Let's look at how these walks can work.

Schedule a Facilities Walk

The "facilities walk" might be top of your list during your first weeks on the job. Think about buying a house: before you sign on the dotted line, realtors will recommend that buyers schedule inspections so that buyers are aware of any physical needs or areas in need of repair. Buyers can then make informed financial decisions: is my offer price reasonable, now that we have learned the house needs a new roof and a septic replacement, and discovered possible mold in the basement? Most buyers would negotiate for a better purchase price or ask for financial credit toward those expensive repairs. Some buyers may back out, turned off by the amount of structural needs, and look for a newer construction with fewer issues.

Doing a building walk is a lot like the inspections process when purchasing a new home, except you're not purchasing this school, and there's no negotiating for credits. The issues uncovered in a facilities walk become items on your to-do list, often urgently. By including the Facilities Director, there is also hope that some of these items can be moved to their "to-do" list, and not added to yours.

Together, you and the Facilities Director can walk every single corner of that building, pointing out and noting the needed repairs. Every missing floor tile, every wall with chipped paint, every leaky ceiling tile, every broken radiator. You can prioritize projects and form a "punch list" of projects to be completed and when—some might be urgent and need attention right away, and some can be completed progressively as the year goes on.

In my case, the Facilities Director and I decided that in terms of larger projects, we'd start with the restrooms; these are common areas that every single student utilizes. We scheduled the facilities team to update them: they repainted, replaced missing doors, and re-tiled the floors. It seems so common sense, yet it hadn't been done in decades. The main foyer was given a new coat of paint and was accented in bright new colors. Several areas of the school that hadn't been touched in years were cleaned, trash was thrown out . . . it was cathartic. We took pictures along the way, and on the first day staff returned that fall, we presented the building's transformation to the faculty, with a focus on the importance of our physical environment. Obviously your school district may not have a facilities director. Your maintenance team might be your sole custodian and you. However, between parent volunteers, and anyone you can drag in who cares about building appearances, at the very least you can make it brighter, more welcoming, and feel fresh in some of the important places in the school setting.

When we start paying attention to the physical environment of our school, it sends a message to the community, students, and staff that someone cares and someone is watching.

Clean Out Those Closets

In addition to having structural issues, some buildings are a literal mess. I'd liken mine to a teenager's bedroom, or the TV show *Hoarders* where piles of paper and boxes of random "stuff" were ubiquitous. Strangely, it wasn't even the current faculty's mess. It had collected over time, and no one "saw" it anymore. They were just working around it. Sometimes we are also just hesitant to dispose of certain things. Since bell bottom jeans have come back in style, maybe so will overhead projectors and ditto machines.

We (me and anyone I could convince to help me) spent that entire summer cleaning out closets, both literally and figuratively. Working in a negative physical environment can have a negative effect on everything. It can trickle down to affect things such as staff attendance, student attendance, parent morale, staff motivation, and community pride. If staff are reporting to work each day in a building that is unclean, unkempt, neglected, with things falling apart such as holes in the walls, chipping paint, missing floor tiles . . . what message does that send to them? To the students and families? I found items in closets that had no reason to exist in the school: wedding photos of employees that no longer worked there, a potty-training kit, holiday decorations that had yellowed and torn over the years. These items were taking up space in a school that was desperate for an organizational overhaul and to be streamlined for organization and efficiency.

Don't Do It On Your Own

Learn every single person at the district—or any—level who can support you with the immediate concerns you are facing. Get to know and build relationships with the maintenance and facilities staff, as they will be essential to helping you improve the building itself. By reaching out to various offices in the district and community, you can establish connections and share your hopes for your school: you need improvements, and you need help. Most people *want* to help; they want to be part of a turnaround story. A makeover!

At first, I reached out to staff for help purely due to need, though I later realized the long-term benefits of this. As an example, the "Team Room," which was the hub of many parent meetings, special education team meetings, and housed our school Psychologist and Social Worker, was looking dingy and disorganized. This room should be warm, welcoming, and above all else, look professional. In this room, staff members hold meetings with parents, discussing their child's academic challenges, and the need for possible special education or placement changes. These conversations should not be happening in a room that looks like an unkempt storage facility! We pictured a coffee maker, some comfortable seating, Kleenex, games, and puzzles for families who brought their youngest children due to lack of childcare. So I reached out to my school Psychologist (whom I did not know) and shared that we were considering painting that room, re-organizing, etc. and would he want to help or pick out the colors? Amazingly enough, he readily agreed to come in on his own time that summer. He grabbed a paint roller and helped paint that room. Other teachers whom I had met or had known previously from my time there as reading coach wanted to help too. Getting them involved not only helped the cleanup process; it also allowed them to retake ownership of their space.

You can have small groups of teachers paint rooms, re-organize, and otherwise "beautify" their spaces. To see so many people come together will provide a great deal of hope. It will also change the "I" to "we" when you share with staff the story of your school's transformation. Rather than hearing the principal stand in front of the staff and take credit for working to "fix their broken school," you can celebrate the efforts of so many that resulted in the benefits to all. Of course, they may know you initiated the updates, but using the term "we" can build a team and create a momentum of getting people on board and feeling true ownership of the school.

Show Off the Upgrades

Upgrades can have an immediate effect on your staff. Teachers will feel proud to report to work each day in a clean, more professional, more welcoming environment. Students will feel excited to come to school each day in a clean and bright environment. And as a result, they may respect the space more. You may find less graffiti on the walls, for example. Even if people don't know why things changed, they will know that things feel changed. And for the better.

Show off your before and after photos at staff meetings and/or in staff newsletters. At our first staff orientation day, we incorporated before and after photos into the presentation. We compared the dirty chipping walls with the new, bright and freshly painted "after" of the same wall. We compared the old bathrooms versus the updated ones. We also made sure to thank the staff members who came in over the summer to contribute to the "after effect." The room erupted into applause—teachers were very happy to see that the building was finally getting some much-needed attention.

Keep the Updates Going

You might have some building issues you need to tackle immediately, and others that will go on your three- or five-year plan. A few years after I made the first improvements, I decided to tackle the playground. We only had a paved blacktop and a giant patch of mud. Games such as hopscotch and Four Square had been painted on the blacktop over the years but had faded, and several wide cracks were running through the pavement, with tall weeds sprouting out of every crack. It was not a nice place for children to play every day. We wrote a grant for some playground equipment and a grant for some paving and sealcoating. We had the equipment installed and had several yards of playground mulch delivered. Once the mud patch had been paved and the blacktop was seal-coated, we had bright, colorful playground games painted on. The before and after pictures of this playground transformation were spectacular.

I had gotten in the habit (after the positive response from my first Orientation Day and the summer transformation pictures) of showing pictures of building improvements that had occurred over the summer when teachers returned for Orientation. The 2-minute video we showed about the playground transformation was so impactful that teachers clapped, cheered, and cried. When looking around the room, it was easy to remember why it is always so important to keep at the forefront of our minds that some of these teachers have worked here, *in this building,* for decades. These teachers started families at this school; they've mourned major losses while working here. This school is *their* home first. Yes, I feel ownership and responsibility, and yes I feel pride, as it's my home now, too, but seeing their "home away from home" get spruced up and improved was impactful to them in a way that gave me goosebumps. If you have pride in where you work, it is much easier to have pride in yourself and what you do.

Nowhere is it stated that principals must upkeep or improve our playgrounds and other outside areas. In fact, when working at a low-performing school, many people might say that the playground should not even matter. There's truth to the fact that prioritization of students' educational experience is paramount, but sometimes to establish that a leader is here for people—students first, staff and families next—it can help to start with easy, uncontroversial wins. Recalcitrant staff may not always like what a leader has to say, but will always respect the fact that a leader is tackling issues that have plagued the building for years. If we start with the points of least resistance, it may reduce the pushback as we head toward points with more resistance. If employees respect the fact that a leader prioritized their work environment, and families see that the leader prioritizes the environment they send their kids to each day, it can help establish a trust that future decisions are made with the best of intentions.

On Board with Your Goals, Not with Your Fan Club

Some of the people clapping and cheering (and crying) about my before and afters were teachers that were not exactly members of my fan club—or seemingly any fan club. Some of these teachers had pushed back on my feedback or complained and griped about evaluations or employee discipline. But in this moment, there was a powerful realization that they respected me, or more likely respected and appreciated *this project* and its impact on our school. This is a powerful realization, too: getting people "on the bus" does not always equal people *liking* us. It's easy to confuse the two. People can be on the bus and share the leader's values and vision toward improving the school but may themselves be change-resistant. Improvement often brings big change along with it, so those slow to adapt will be slow to please. A teacher doesn't need to agree with every one of your decisions to share your overall vision for school improvement and be willing and able to do what it takes.

Final Thoughts

The physical appearance of a school isn't just superficial—it has an impact on staff and student morale, and the school's perception by the community. When the building is taken care of, and staff, community, and students feel that someone cares and someone is watching out for them, it makes a difference. It might seem superficial to worry about paint when there are so many concerns to tackle, but sometimes we have to start at a basic level if we ever want to climb the summit. Often it is the first and most visible place to start. It is fun to see people look at the visible alterations and know they are thinking "Wow, things are happening around here."

3

Structure, Structure, Structure

One of the most common negative comments that people make about a school is that the kids are "outta control." In the years prior to me being hired as a Turnaround Principal at my school, substitute teachers would call the district Human Resource Office after one day and request to never be placed at the school again.

One day in June, after I had accepted the position as principal but before my official start date in July, school was still in session and the school was on its third principal of the year. The Elementary Executive Director suggested that she and I visit the school so I could get a "snapshot" of how things were going. As we walked the building, I was shocked by many of the things we witnessed. A couple moments worth noting:

♦ We walked into a large room that looked to be a Computer Lab. About four or five students were alone, playing games on different computers, completely unsupervised. We asked, "What's going on in here?" and the students told us they'd been kicked out of their classrooms so they were playing on the computer. *Did their teachers know they were here? Has anyone been assigned to supervise this room? Who's responsible for keeping these students safe?*

♦ We walked into the Bus Room at the end of the day, where students awaited their buses to head home. Students were all over the room; it was impossible to discern which students were in which bus line. One boy

DOI: 10.4324/9781003321323-5

was recklessly running around doing backflips. I asked one of the Teacher Assistants who was monitoring the room, "What's going on in here?" She said, "Oh, that's Joe's responsibility, but he's not here today." *So, is anyone assigned to cover for Joe today, to supervise the children on that bus?*

Is It Really the Students . . . Or Something More?

On the way out the door with my new boss, I started to get lightheaded. Did I really sign up to try and fix all of this? Is it too late to say "just kidding!" and return to my previous job? But for all the anxiety and disbelief that the visit had caused, there was a real sense of determination setting in, too. This was fixable, and I believed we could do it. I knew right away that of course the kids were not to blame. There were certainly some behaviors that needed attention. But overall, what was staring me in the face was not strictly a "student behaviors are out of control!" problem. It was a lack of structure problem, a culture problem.

When you are dealing with behavior issues in your school, start with the adults, not the students. Whenever we want to change student behavior, we must first change adult behavior (Whitaker, 2018). If we only address the student behaviors we're seeing—the back flip, the disorder—then we're going to find ourselves on a hamster wheel, exhausted from treating the symptoms and not the root cause of the problem. In my case, the root case was lack of structures, which had been manifesting itself as out-of-control children. But in reality, it was an out-of-control system.

Examine Each Part of the School Day: Arrival, Leaving, Breaks, and More

It takes time, but a complete examination of each portion of the school day might be in order. Look at every area of whole-school operations: Morning Arrival, Lunch/Cafeteria, Hallway Passage, Bathroom Breaks . . . everything can be examined and revisited.

Here is an example of working backwards to figure out where things are going wrong. In my case, I started with the Bus Room—the area where students waited for their buses to arrive at the end of the school day. I asked questions such as:

◆ *How are students getting to the Bus Room each day?*
◆ *How long are they expected to wait in the Bus Room?*
◆ *What is the layout of the Bus Room once students have entered? How do they get to their bus line?*
◆ *What happens when students exit the Bus Room doors: How do they remain safely in line as they walk to board their bus?*
◆ *How do we know all bus students are accounted for?*

Reflecting on these questions shined a light on some very simple solutions. First: students were being "sent" to the Bus Room. There was no actual structure in place for *escorting* or supervising students to the Bus Room, much less ensuring that they made it there safely. As it was currently playing out, it was a free for all. I drafted a Dismissal Procedure to be put in place on the first day, which required all classroom teachers to line their students up in two lines at the end of the day: a Bus line and a Walkers' line. ("Walkers" refers to any student who does not ride a bus—their parents pick them up or they walk home.) Teachers were to escort their classes in those two lines down to the main foyer each day, stopping at the exterior door, Door 2, right by the Bus Room. They'd then pass the Bus students into the bus room and walk out Door 2. By escorting the students down to the Bus Room, it ensured that at no time would students be alone in the hallway. They'd have adult supervision until the moment they entered that room.

Consider which portions of the school day aren't going smoothly in your building. Work backwards to create a list like the above—what questions can you ask yourself that will help you devise a solution? You may not have a Bus Room, but potentially you have locations, transitions, and times of the day that can be problematic. If at a middle school, students race down the hallway between classes and amazingly still arrive late, how does this prepare them for success in their next class? Working to reduce unstructured and unsupervised time is essential to a calm and organized school environment.

Thinking ahead to potential traffic jams and long, Disney World-type lines in the hallway, I also created a "Staggered Dismissal Schedule" where every five minutes another cluster of classrooms on each floor should pass from their classrooms toward the foyer. The staggering of the dismissal times ensured that all 23 classrooms didn't exit into the hallway at the same time, causing a commotion. Even the very best teachers would be challenged to keep children safe and orderly waiting in hallway lines that long with that much stimulation. Staggering the dismissal created short bursts of short lines which were very fast-moving and efficient.

As for the actual Bus Room, I stacked that room with supervision. Every single person who was not attached to a classroom was charged with supervising one corner or another of that room. Specialist teachers (PE, Music), Teacher Assistants, Resource Teachers, the Wellness Team (Social Worker, Psychologist), Related Service Providers (Speech & Language, Occupational Therapy), and Instructional Coaches were all assigned a role in the safe, orderly loading of buses. Two to three adults were assigned to each bus line, and students were to sit and read until their bus arrived. Two adults were stationed outside as "Stopping Points" to ensure that the long lines of students remained intact and that students behaved safely en route to their bus as they neared the street. Wellness Team members were stationed in the hallway to guide students into the Bus Room at the correct volume. I was not sure what these professionals were all doing in years past during dismissal. Paperwork? Phone calls? Perhaps they were taking a moment to catch up on a task before leaving for the day. Not having a classroom of children to dismiss, they could easily go unaccounted for. These folks weren't intentionally lazy or unsupportive, they just needed direction.

Bus Room staff collected "Bus Tickets" with student names on them, so that we had a daily accurate count of exactly which students loaded the bus each day. Staff took attendance on the way out the door, and then bus staff took attendance again once the students loaded the bus.

Handling the Naysayers

I did have one of my new instructional coaches tell me that dismissal is not in her contractual job description and that she did not need to support loading buses. I replied that dismissal was All Hands On Deck. She scoffed at first: "But my job is about data and instruction. Coaches at other schools don't help with dismissal." I was surprised. We didn't have time or room for That's Not My Job-ers. Especially from someone whom I considered a leader in our school. I reminded her that part of her job *was* building trust with the teachers. How would the teachers feel if they knew that every member of the school community was committed to getting students home safely—except for one? She eventually softened to the idea, as I know she truly was committed to turning the school around. This was a mindset issue for her. She was an instructional leader in our school and would have to shift her old mindset that compartmentalized "instruction" and "operations."

How can you deal with staff members who aren't as invested in Bus Duty or Cafeteria Duty? Consider trying to create a sense of pride and belonging within that group. For example, we started to have fun contests in the Bus Room while waiting to load buses. I assigned two or three staff members to each bus, and they were responsible for recording attendance, collecting bus tickets, and maintaining order in those bus lines. As the afternoon wore on, it became harder for the children to sustain sitting in lines, reading books, and waiting. So we'd have contests and competitions between Bus Lines. For example, we'd say "best scary face!" and make a huge production on the microphone about which Bus Line had the best scary faces. We'd choose a winner together, and I would announce that "Mr. Connor's line" or "Miss McGee's line" was the winner. Whatever the contest (best fake sleeping, best silly pose, best whatever!) we'd announce it on the morning announcements the following day. I'd make sure to attribute the bus line to the supervisors . . . "Narrowly beating out Mr. Connor's bus line for

Best Scary Faces was Bus 33, Mrs. Potter and Miss Carrington's line! See if our defending champs can keep the title today in the Bus Room. . ."

You can also make an effort to show the team in the Bus Room or Cafeteria how much you appreciate them and how much you're depending on them. I showed my appreciation in part by purchasing rain ponchos for all Bus Room Supervisors. On rainy days we all wore them together. The front had our school logo and the back reads "TEAM BUS DUTY" in bright gold letters. We took a group photo the first day wearing them. I've found little gestures like this go a very long way. Bus Duty isn't traditionally cool. It isn't a task that others are envious of. But we made it feel like an exclusive club, like everyone who wasn't in the Bus Room at the end of the day was missing out.

Repeat and Model Expectations

You can't just show something one time and expect it to stick. It's important to repeat, model, re-teach, and reward. Consistency is key. We repeated Bus Room expectations constantly; we taught and re-taught the correct way to enter the Bus Room, outlined the flow of traffic we expected students to follow, and rewarded positive Bus Room behavior by handing out PBIS tickets, announcing the "Best Bus Line of the Day!" on the morning announcements the next day. It was a labor of love, consistent every single day. I was a constant presence in that Bus Room, and still am, ten years later. Model, Model, Model. Be present, be visible. Potentially the school has had years of doing the wrong thing, so it will take practice and consistency to relearn the right thing.

We also created a safe system for dismissing buses out onto the street by stationing staff in two key locations en route to the street. Students not only had staff escorting them outside, but also had two additional adults stopping and looking to reward and compliment excellent bus line behavior. We created a system of loading the furthest bus first. This eliminated the student lines from crossing and becoming a jumbled mess of children so close to the street. Once the furthest bus is loaded, we move up and load the next one, then the next, until we are left with the closest bus.

Small details like this make a huge difference. You can choreograph the entire dismissal down to the minute. Leave nothing to chance; put systems in place to ensure order. My bus room was no longer a chaotic mess. If Joe is absent, there are at least three other adults assigned to ensure supervision is consistent in his bus line.

I remember standing in the Bus Room one afternoon, mid-dismissal, when one of my most notoriously negative teachers approached me. As she was complaining to me about a situation that happened to her earlier in the day, she interrupted herself to say, "Wow. Look at this Bus Room. You really fixed this. I'll give you that." Rare praise from a teacher who was more comfortable complaining than complimenting . . . I'll take it!

An unintended but entirely welcomed side effect of having so many hands on deck during dismissal was that it increased the amount of students that staff members were building relationships with. Math coaches were creating "fist bump" routines with students walking down the street to their bus. Our Speech Pathologist was getting and giving hugs to so many students who equated her to being the "friendly face as they walked out the door." Normally she would only know the students on her caseload, but she was now a local celebrity.

Final Thoughts

By looking at structures and routines for entering and leaving the building, lunchtime, and more, you can slowly but surely reduce the student behavior issues during those times. Work backwards to figure out the issues, create better systems, and then keep teaching and modeling expectations, getting all staff on board. The perception that the kids at your school are "outta control" will decrease. Eventually the common areas with large congregations of students will begin to be safe, orderly, and very much under control.

II

It's All About Your Teachers

4

Getting (and Onboarding) Better Staff

In education, many programs and initiatives come and go. We often think, *If we can just get the latest foundational skills program here at school, I bet we'll see an increase in our reading achievement.* Yet walking in this new role as Turnaround Principal, it was like a lightbulb switched on for me. I realized, *It is people, not programs, that determine the quality of a school* (Whitaker, 2020).

It all comes down to your people. There are really just two ways to significantly improve a school: 1) hire better teachers, and 2) improve the ones you have.

Getting better teachers and improving the ones you have is not a quick, overnight process. Getting better teachers means that there needs to be a vacancy to hire new teachers into. The work that goes into clearing the vacancy—coaching and support, documentation, progressive discipline, coaching out, etc.—can be all-consuming. Yet that work must happen at the same time that we're dedicated to the second part, improving the teachers we have. This chapter will focus on the first part, hiring; the next chapter will focus on improvement.

DOI: 10.4324/9781003321323-7

Hire Effective Teachers

One single teaching position—one teacher!—can affect hundreds of children's lives for the better. The teacher is the number one variable in the classroom (Whitaker, 2020). Where some students may still succeed in spite of a poor teacher, the majority of students may succeed only because of a great teacher—perhaps many great teachers! Particularly in schools and districts where negative factors such as trauma and poverty are highly prevalent, it's more important than ever to ensure that the *very best teachers* are in front of these children every single day. Having a vacancy open up is the embodiment of possibility, hope, and great things to come.

When you begin hiring, remember that the goal is not for the new person to fall in line. It's for them to start a new line (Whitaker, 2020). Each and every hire you bring into a school can help enrich it. This is true for every classroom teacher, every specialist, every administrator, coach, and Teacher Assistant. Each person has the ability to propel the school higher on our journey—or, if you don't hire well, to bring it further down. So how do we hire effectively? Here are a few strategies.

1. Craft Better Interview Questions

When interviewing staff, there are questions that can give us insight into the candidate's knowledge of standards, lesson planning, behavior management systems—standard interview questions that educators across the nation would recognize. Why not add others? At my school, we added a couple of questions at the end of each interview which we felt could "make or break" a certain candidate: *In what ways would you contribute to our building culture and climate? How do you see yourself being a leader?* This has uncovered some insightful, and otherwise potentially missed, information about our candidates.

The latter question is particularly important for schools in turnaround mode. As mentioned previously, we had done a lot of work with a grant application and wanted to build teacher-leaders. Teachers had started taking the lead on facilitating grade-level planning and supporting/mentoring new teachers.

There were so many opportunities for teachers in my building to lead. Without staff who were ready to do so, we wouldn't have been able to pull off so many improvements. So we asked that question, *How do you see yourself being a leader*? We found it so interesting to see how various job candidates would respond. No answers were obviously "right or wrong," they just always elicited vastly different responses.

One of my brand-new hires, Lara, had answered that question particularly well during her interview over the summer. She then spent the entire year with us, immersed in our culture of promoting teacher leadership. She was a wonderful teacher, extremely thoughtful and conscientious. She was the type of hire that made all of the efforts involved in "making room for your best teachers" worth it. All the progressive discipline, all the documentation—to end up with a teacher like Lara in front of our students was the goal.

Since Lara had been hired after the cutoff date of August 1st, she was forced to re-apply to her same job if she wanted to keep it at the year's end. Of course, we wanted to hire her back—she was excellent—but out of an abundance of caution she applied to a few other jobs in the district as well.

We interviewed her, and again concluded with that question: *How do you see yourself being a leader in our building?* She told us about the ways she had grown throughout her first year as a teacher, and the ways she saw herself taking the lead in the future were she to return. She had a solid interview, as well as a terrific first year with us, and when we offered her the job back, she accepted.

That night, as all of the interview committees in our district were deliberating and sending job offers, I was on the phone with a colleague of mine, a principal at a school across the city. I asked him, "Did you fill all of your positions tonight? Anyone interesting?" He told me of some of his hires, then added, "Man we were bummed we lost out on our top candidate for fifth grade, though. We interviewed this awesome girl, Lara. At the end of the interview when we asked her if she had any questions for us, she asked us, 'What opportunities would you have for me to be a leader in your school?' It blew us away! What a great question. The team loved her. But she accepted another job offer. Shame—she was our favorite!"

2. Ask for Concrete Rather Than Theoretical Responses

Here is another trick for improving your interview questions. Stop asking questions theoretically (ex: "How would you handle a parent who comes to you with a major complaint?" "How will you use grade level standards and WIDA standards to differentiate and plan for instruction?") or you may always get "canned" answers. Instead, start asking them with an expectation for a more concrete answer with evidence of past or current practice. Examples: "Tell about a time you worked with an upset parent regarding a complaint or a problem. How would you handle things differently, if at all?" "How do you currently plan for differentiated instruction using grade level standards and WIDA Can-Do descriptors? Have you had any challenges or successes in planning that you'd like to share?" This way, candidates are not reciting buzz words or things that they know they should say but are forced to say how they *already do* something. (For recent college graduates who have no prior teaching experience, we allow them to say how they *would* do something. We usually frame it a bit differently so that they can talk about their current internship experience with adding how they plan to adapt/adjust when they have their own classroom. It still helps us gauge how much independence or ownership they've had in each particular area.)

I remember when I was preparing for my first principal interview. I was so excited and determined to get the job. And with zero prior administrative experience, I was so proud to have made the final two candidates. Ultimately the job went to someone who had a few years as Assistant Principal under his belt. But I attribute my success in that interview process to the fact that my mentor prepared me for the interview by saying, don't tell them what you *would* do. Tell them *what you are already doing*. They will be able to picture you doing those things at their school and be able to determine if you are the best fit.

I researched that school before the interview and knew that they had a grade 5 vacancy and a large population of Multilingual

Learners (MLLs). When asked what I would do first if I were hired, I answered, "Well, I see that we have a grade 5 classroom vacancy. First thing we need to do is hire the right person for that job so we're fully staffed." I shared with them that as a teacher and a reading coach, I felt that we'd need to hire a candidate with strong classroom management, knowledge of the current reading curriculum, and an English as a Second Language certification. I answered a question about instructional goals by using their current performance data to set a realistic goal and explain what I'm working on with teachers in my role as Reading Coach at my current school to support MLLs, that we could bring to their school and expand.

When I learned I didn't get the job, I was emotional because I'd had my heart set on it. But the world had other plans for me as I ultimately went on to 1) do a year as an Assistant Principal which I realized as I was doing it, was *so* necessary and should be a requirement before becoming principal, and 2) end up a year later as the principal at the school where I am now. However, the Elementary School Executive Director shared some feedback with me after that first principal interview experience. She said, the committee loved your knowledge of their school and really liked the way you had already started planning to get to work. She explained that they, and she, ultimately went with the candidate with more experience and to "keep your head up, you have a lot to offer."

I tell this story because it taught me a lot about what to look for in an interview, and what types of questions yield deeper information than just surface-level questions. When candidates are able to place themselves (figuratively) in the position they are seeking and tell you how they do their jobs, you are able to see more clearly if this person is the right fit. The interview shifts from picturing an imaginary scenario, to garnering a mental image of this person as your new (fill in the blank) teacher.

3. Sell Candidates on Your School

Remember that an interview goes two ways—you're not just seeing if you like the candidate. The candidates are also seeing if your school is a fit for them. So don't forget to leave time in the interview to sell the candidate on your school's story. I started this a few years into our turnaround journey. It has become such a special part of the interview that my team members now join me in telling candidates the narrative of our school's uplift.

We keep it brief—after all, interviews are generally timed with people trying to stick to a schedule—but we cover the fact that our school has been on a transformative journey, and we highlight some special moments we've had along the way. We share stories about the way things used to be (substitutes requesting never to return, students walking out of class), and how our school is on a mission to transform itself and how important every new staff member is to our journey. We share our teacher leadership opportunities, our culture and climate committee events, and our progress toward hitting achievement goals. What is most touching to me is how the teachers on my hiring committee have taken on the ownership of telling our school's story. It used to be that I would be the narrator, and they'd nod, adding bits and pieces. Now, they practically trip over each other to tell job candidates about the positive journey of improvement our school has been on.

Each member of my hiring committee has been going through the process of turning our school around with me, and it's gratifying and emotional to see the care, pride, and protectiveness in their voices as they share with job candidates how special they feel our school is. In most cases, this portion of the interview inspires the candidate to share that they'd very much like to be part of something special and ask us more questions. Sharing our school's story actually helps us to detect a candidate's fit; those who respond enthusiastically and seem ready to get on board are far more likely to be "on the bus" once they arrive. It's fair to let a candidate know right off the bat that they are potentially signing on to a school that is on a serious mission to improve! Better to know sooner than later if someone is looking to hide out, or if someone is excited and motivated by being a positive component of a school in transformation.

4. Bring In the Joy

Speaking of being positive: How might your candidates bring joy to your school? A few years into our school's transformation journey, we were interviewing for a fifth grade ESL classroom teacher position. Our two candidates were vastly different:

Candidate A:
- ◆ Was currently an Assistant Principal
- ◆ Had several years' experience teaching middle school and grade 5
- ◆ Was certified in teaching English Language Learners
- ◆ Excellent references

Candidate B:
- ◆ Had just finished teacher preparatory programs, had never taught his own class before
- ◆ Was not yet certified in teaching English Language Learners but was willing to continue his education and get that certification
- ◆ Had just participated in an intensive year-long program which allowed him to shadow a fifth-grade teacher (whom the team knew and had an excellent reputation)
- ◆ Excellent references

For all purposes, one might think that Candidate A should get the job due to her experience. Her interview was good; she had a lot of knowledge of teaching ELLs and was very smart about the ways she used data to inform her instruction. When we asked her why she wanted to switch over from being an administrator to being a fifth-grade teacher, she looked directly at me and said, "I'm sure you don't even need to ask. It's a stressful job! I need a change."

It's an honest answer and not necessarily disqualifying, but it landed strangely for my team. She seemed like she had *been there, done that* and was looking for a break. We couldn't put our finger on why we weren't in love with this candidate. We'd be lucky to hire someone with this hard-to-find certification! We'd be lucky to hire someone who knows how to manage tough behaviors and is familiar with the "big picture" of how a school operates.

Candidate B's interview was also good. He answered all of our questions with reasonable, thoughtful replies and shared his experiences shadowing his cooperating teacher. What stood out to us was when we asked him what qualities he thought were most important in being a fifth-grade teacher, he replied, "The J-factor!" When asked what that meant, he replied, "Joy." He then explained how important he feels it is to bring happiness and joy to the classroom.

His energy and enthusiasm were palpable. The team really struggled with our decision at first because what we *wanted* to do seemed to contradict the smarter choice on paper. Ultimately, we unanimously felt that we wanted to work with Candidate B. He was aligned with our vision for school improvement and shared our common values. We wanted to be around him. *We wanted him to start a new line.*

We offered the job to Candidate B and he accepted. He delivered on his promise to bring joy into the classroom. He stepped up and became a leader across the board; he was facilitating professional development to staff within his first two years. His classroom was often engaged in project-based learning, constructing towers with cups during a measurement unit, hatching baby chickens during a science unit, strutting around the school to show the entire building that they were put together because *they were the best students!*

Two months into Candidate B's first year with us, after getting home from our annual Fall Harvest Festival family engagement event, he emailed my Assistant Principal and me the following:

"I just wanted to reach out and thank you both for believing in me on June 1, 2017. *[The date of his job interview.]* I love my students, I love my colleagues, and I love this school. Tonight was thrilling in all the right ways and I'm glad to have found a school that I can call home.

With Gratitude,

Mike"

To this day, this particular hiring decision is one that our team often uses as a "landmark case" when we deliberate during the interview process. *Teaching and learning should bring joy.* A candidate's fit and their qualifications both matter. What also matters, but is decidedly harder to spot, is their potential. During our yearly hiring fair process, our team now specifically calls out ways to determine if a candidate would bring the J-factor to our school. A perfect example of how if you hire correctly your goal is to have your school become more like your new teacher than to have your new teacher become like your school. It's hard to have too much Joy in any workplace—especially one working to make a difference in the lives of young people.

Onboarding Matters

Once you establish who your new staff members are, you can involve your leadership team in creating a "New Teacher Orientation," which you can weave into back-to-school week. New Teacher Orientation is for any staff member new to the building, not just teachers new to the profession. Year one or year 24, it makes no difference. The orientation can help preserve and build on the culture you've established and the progress you've made. You have created so many internal structures and processes and want to ensure that no new staff member feels confused or reverts back to the "way things used to be" at the last school they worked at. You can celebrate new staff with tokens of appreciation, such as mugs that say "My Boss Thinks I'm a Big Deal!" or "Proud Member of an Awesome Team!" Our goal in doing so is to begin right from the start, to grow a sense of pride and belonging in our new staff members. It's the culmination of the momentum we generated in the interview, when we shared our school's transformation goals and story.

This Place Is a Vibe

How many teachers honestly look forward to Orientation Day? Most dread the day where their summer vacation ends, and they are inundated with new district mandates, new initiatives and programs. No one likes watching the medical training videos that haven't been updated since we began our careers. As much as teachers can love their jobs, there is something about Orientation Day that can cause even the most dedicated teachers to grumble and complain, which is doubly sad since we start the year undefeated! When focused on creating a momentum and a feeling of pride in the workplace, I started to view Orientation Day as an "event." Each year I choose a theme for the day, often closely tied to recent successes or events at our school. During the day, I weave the theme into all aspects of the presentations and build momentum toward a big reveal at the end of the day where the whole staff gets a t-shirt. This may seem like a small thing, but it has become our tradition. The t-shirt often has a motivational saying on it that encapsulates the day's theme. Some past t-shirts say "Never Give Up: Great Things Take Time!" and "Stay Positive. Work Hard. Make It Happen." Each year, as the day comes to a close, I'll pick an upbeat song and play it while we reveal and distribute the new staff t-shirts.

A couple years ago, we did such a great job of setting the tone that one of our new hires, a young teacher, looked around the room and said to an established teacher, "The place is a vibe, huh?" The veteran teacher came to me to say, "You'll love this. Guess what Shay said during Back to School—she called it 'a vibe.'" I really did love it. Shay succinctly captured exactly what we had been aiming to do with orientation. This place IS a vibe, Shay! Thank you for being a part of it. The hard work that so many of us have been putting in, the "above and beyond" mindset that so many people had internalized, the celebratory nature of our staff welcoming new people—I felt proud knowing that new hires were coming to my school and feeling that *this place is a vibe*. What a difference from the days when nobody wanted to work at our school. What we were doing was working. If the teachers are feeling this way, the positivity will find a way to trickle down to the students. Happy teachers, happy students. It all connects. By the way, as a reader of this book, feel free to hand your faculty This Place Is A Vibe t-shirts next year!

Just last year, we had a larger-than-normal transition of staff. Several staff members relocated, some retired, and some pursued job opportunities in a different certification area. I was nervous that we were at a brand new beginning and might lose some of our momentum that we had built over the past eight years. In planning for the opening of schools, I decided our Orientation Day theme would celebrate and embrace the amount of staff turnover, rather than allowing it to be a challenge. Last year's theme was "It's a Brand New Day." We celebrated our new staff members and honored those we missed, who had been there for so much of our transformational journey. We started the day as we always do, celebrating milestones or notable occasions that happened over the summer. We shared pictures of Shay getting engaged in Puerto Rico, celebrated a staff member moving, mentioned a few staff members who had children starting college and another who was newly pregnant. I then shared a slide with a Dan Millman quote: "The secret of change is to focus all of your energy not on fighting the old but on building the new." The image associated with the quote was of a person who had climbed the mountain and was looking out, over the hills and trees, to a beautiful sunrise. The person's arms were outstretched, giving off a celebratory feel.

We then dug into the meat and potatoes of the day: updated bell times, the employee handbook, IEP/504 updates, restraint training, health updates, instructional priorities—you know the drill. Whenever I could incorporate the words "brand new," "new day," or "fresh start" into a slide, I did. I stepped way past "subtle" and entered "hitting them over the head with it" territory in terms of messaging. At the end of the slide show, we returned to the same quote, and the song "It's a New Day" by Will.I.Am began to play over the speakers of the auditorium. Over the musical introduction, I told my team: "My challenge to you for this year is to focus all of your energy on the new while honoring and remembering the people we've worked with along the way. Remember that our secret is out: This is a great school with great people. Take pride in how far we have come and have faith in how far we are still going to go." The final slide revealed our t-shirt for the year which said "It's a Brand New Day on the South Side" and had our slogan across the back.

The little things we say and do carry so much weight. When the principal sneezes, the whole school catches a cold (Whitaker, 2020). Make sure you're spreading something positive, not a virus of negativity. If the principal comes across as motivated and excited, even if they're worried or unsure on the inside, the whole school will take notice and feel taken care of.

If we can keep ensuring that our teaching positions are filled by great teachers and stay clear and consistent with communication, we will continue to attract the right people. It's a self-sustaining cycle. Both new, early-career teachers *and* veteran/established teachers who are looking to make a difference have a place. Retaining and hiring the best teachers has to be our highest leverage point.

Final Thoughts

Hiring effective new teachers is key to turning around a school. We can ensure that our interview questions reveal the right things about the candidates, and we can ensure we're selling the candidates on our school in return. Once new teachers are hired, our goal is to have the school become more like the new teachers and not have the new teachers become more like the school. Finally, we can't overlook the importance of onboarding and new teacher orientation to create our vibe.

5

Letting Teachers Go and Improving the Ones You Have

One of the saddest parts of a building leader's job is walking into a classroom and witnessing valuable instructional time being wasted. Even sadder is when the occurrence is habitual and not just a one-off. An uncomfortable part of a principal's job is having to manage poor teaching that has not improved over time despite coaching, supports, and interventions. I once heard a district administrator use the expression "it's like watering rocks and hoping they grow" to describe situations in which she had coached and supported teachers only to see absolutely no growth or improvement. Worse still, no *desire* to grow or improve. I often think back to my first years as principal as being really, really consumed with watering my rocks.

Facing the "Quit but Stayed" Phenomenon

New teachers, teachers having a rough year, teachers struggling to learn new programs or new technology . . . bring it on. It is our job to help them! Coaching, observations/feedback cycles, peer mentors—this is the name of the game. What I'm specifically talking about is when a teacher has "quit but stayed," a term I learned by necessity as I walked the halls of my turnaround

DOI: 10.4324/9781003321323-8

school the first couple years. Maybe you have those teachers at your school, too.

These employees exist in every type of workplace. People who Quit but Stayed are people who are physically present in their classrooms, show up for work every day, but mentally are "over it" or phoning it in. They have lost their passion or joy for teaching and put forth the least amount of effort possible, while remaining gainfully employed and collecting a paycheck each week.

I remember during my first year talking to a veteran administrator in the district who had worked at my school many years ago. I mentioned how shocked I was at how rough things were in Wendy's classroom, and he said, "Oh Wendy retired years ago!" I corrected him, "No, Wendy is still working. She teaches fourth grade." He said, "Yes I know, but she retired years ago. Problem is, she never made it official and still shows up. But mentally, she's been done for years." Wow. He had nailed it.

And this was happening as if it were acceptable. I couldn't laugh about it, although he meant his comments to be humorous. I couldn't stop thinking of the students assigned to Wendy's classroom whose days were ticking by, learning next to nothing due to lack of any quality instruction and interventions. The children were out of their seats, being given "busy work," and receiving little to no grade-level projects or activities.

The Quit but Stayed phenomenon can happen for several reasons, usually slowly over time. When a school's culture and climate are miserable, good teachers want to leave and work somewhere with better conditions. This is exactly what I was encountering. We were left with several employees who had little to no motivation to leave, whose reputations precluded them from faring well at an interview for another job in the district, and who would be at my school forever unless I effectively addressed their poor practice. I was also worried about the average and mediocre classrooms that had no clear role models anymore, no motivation to strive for improvement, and worse, below average to downright poor teachers who were getting a good salary, coasting by day to day, hiding in plain sight, mentally checked out. My good teachers with model classrooms were growing frustrated, witnessing their colleagues taking exorbitant amounts of sick days per year, facing no consequences for lack of preparation and poor classroom management. We were in dangerous waters.

Early on, when joined by members of my district Teaching & Learning team for an instructional learning walk, I'd try to avoid these classrooms at all costs—pay no attention to the man behind the curtain! Everything is going great over here! I was initially concerned that if they saw some of these poor teachers' classrooms, with scant evidence of student engagement, they'd think *"oh wow, we never should have hired Courtney. Look at what's going on under her nose!"* But after continually guiding district officials away from these classrooms, it eventually dawned on me that these rooms are exactly where I *should* be bringing my team. First of all, I will gladly accept the help. If there is a way to rejuvenate teaching with some of my staff who have Quit but Stayed, I'll take all suggestions. Second, it makes our *best* teachers nervous or anxious when district staff walk through their classrooms . . . why am I *protecting* my poor performers, who are bad for children? Why am I making them *more* comfortable by avoiding their classrooms?

Our goal should be to make teachers who are taking advantage of the system—by quitting but staying—as uncomfortable as possible.

Change or Leave

When people feel uncomfortable, they can either change or they can leave. Discomfort is a catalyst to get people moving. Of course, we'd love it if they changed! We'd be overjoyed if our poorest teachers started teaching effective lessons and speaking kindly to their students. And, if they aren't willing or able to do that, we'd love it if they left. *Change, or leave.*

This "change or leave" theory isn't something to take lightly. If someone is an excellent teacher but disagrees with you and challenges you at faculty meetings, you don't need them to leave. It's not about personal relationships or feelings. It's that we can't waste so much water on our school's rocks. The hard reality is that poor classroom practices mean children are not getting the education they deserve. If supporting and coaching checked-out teachers is taking up the lion's share of your time, are the mediocre classrooms and good teachers getting any of your attention?

Be Relentless in Documenting Extreme Cases

There are supports that administrators put in place when observing a poor teaching practice (a performance improvement plan, coaching and support, peer mentoring, and so on). But you can also relentlessly document every instance when student safety and well-being are at risk. If teacher behavior shows a pattern of neglect, we can refer the incident to a district Human Resources office, which might provoke a "hearing" to take place. Hearings might include the district Chief Human Resource Officer, a lawyer from the teachers' union, a lawyer to support you, the teacher in question, and you, as the principal. It's often a negative and uncomfortable experience, especially because the hearings occur *during the school day*. I remember many times I'd have to find coverage for the teacher to attend the hearing in the first place! ("Hi Stacey, yeah, so I know we both have that meeting downtown at 11:15 this morning; I'm going to ask Ben to pop in and cover your classroom. What time were you planning on leaving here to head over? Oh okay, 11:00. I'll make sure he's here so you're not late. Great. See you at the hearing.") Often, the teacher and I would return to work after an emotional or combative "hearing," and we had no choice but to move forward with our professional lives as if everything were normal.

Make sure the right person is the one that's uncomfortable (Whitaker, 2020). With the structure for employee discipline and the hearing process, it was *me* who felt uncomfortable! Over time, however, it was a lot easier to feel *extremely* comfortable at these meetings because I started to care less about the awkward feelings between the teacher and me and just focus on why we were there. We have to stay rooted in the fact that behind each hearing is an incident—or several—where either one child or a classroom of children are not getting a fair deal, or worse. Stay focused on who really matters.

In some school districts, it is extremely rare for a teacher to be terminated. The process is lengthy and understandably sides with the teacher every step of the way. Many principals gave me advice when I was starting out such as, "Don't bother writing everything up. Nothing ever happens." This advice was based on their own experiences, and I understood they were trying to save me some time. Or maybe they said that so they didn't have to do the work necessary to make a difference in the school. Certainly there were times that I would address an incident "off the record," such as tardiness, lack of preparation for a data meeting—minor daily occurrences. These things, until they became habitual or stood in the way of student progress, were mainly adult problems. But when student welfare or academic success was in question, I pursued it.

With the theory of change/discomfort in mind, these hearings resulted in a lot of movement over time. Due to frustration with being called downtown for hearings and legitimate fears about suspension or job loss, my poorest teachers took measures to relocate. What that looked like varied, depending on how close to retirement teachers were or their success at job interviews elsewhere. Four teachers took early retirement. Two requested an internal transfer. Two interviewed out of district and left. One teacher was scheduled to have a hearing with the school board for possible termination and took an early retirement deal.

As much as we might disagree with allowing a poor teacher to voluntarily transfer to another school (all it does is transfer a thorn from my side to my colleague's) or take an early retirement rather than having to face the school board for egregious behavior towards children, the end result was best for my students. Positions that were held up by the wrong people could now be posted and filled with the right people. When people feel uncomfortable, they either change or leave.

I mentioned "adult problems," and I think it's worth expanding on that, too. In the big picture, adult problems are better problems to have than student problems, because we're in the business of educating our students. They are our top priority, and keeping them safe, secure, growing, and thriving is our goal. That said, adult problems can be sneaky. Employee interpersonal relations can seem like "adult drama" and it's easy to categorize these issues as something the adults will just have to deal with on their own. But I have learned over and over again that every single issue that happens within my building ultimately falls on me to either handle, ignore, or mishandle. It's that simple—*and* that overwhelming!

When to Give a Gentle Push

Sometimes, making room for the best people isn't as cut and dry as documenting failure to do their job and entering into a tedious "progressive discipline" battle. For example, I had a teacher, let's call her Barbara, who really wasn't happy for whatever reason, be it personal or professional, and it was bleeding into her daily attitude and interactions with her colleagues. Her first language was complaining. At first, it was easy to shrug off, but it grew more and more every year. Barbara's second language was taking everything personally. Although bilingualism is an asset, these two languages together were a lethal combination.

If we held a grade level planning meeting on looking at our math data and targeting some areas for improvement, Barbara would stare me or my math coach right in the face and ask with an offended tone, "Are you saying I'm not already *doing* that?" It was always awkward for everyone in the room. My go-to response was always positive, "No, of course not Barbara, this isn't personal. We're simply reviewing some best practices to keep these ideas fresh. . ." or something similar, just to keep the peace.

When a staff member was recognized at a faculty meeting for outstanding achievement on the state assessment, Barbara announced loudly, "My data was good, too!" It was embarrassing and again, awkward for everyone in the room. Again, to keep the peace, I remember jumping in with "oh yes, definitely, thank you to EVERYONE who is doing x, y, z . . . Barbara you also do a terrific job with. . ." and the initial person who was being celebrated was soon forgotten.

Staff members started to approach me, asking for private meetings, telling me that Barbara had been so *rude* or so *mean* to them. The incidents were all benign enough to shake off as "that's just Barbara being Barbara," and it was sometimes hard to tell which things I should get involved with and which staff disagreements I should not touch with a ten-foot pole. Yet the negativity and toxic climate on the second floor was growing, despite all of our efforts to the contrary. We'd been bringing in fantastic new hires, changing our school environment by increasing positivity, increasing our community engagement, and yet a simple personality clash on the second floor was causing my best teachers to feel bad.

In the spring, there were several back-to-back staff complaints of incidents that revolved around Barbara, and I decided to do something drastic that I had never done before—I wrote Barbara an unsolicited letter of recommendation. In that letter, I listed every professional obligation that Barbara was responsible for and noted the things that Barbara did well, such as classroom management, adherence to deadlines, and scaffolding instruction for her English Language Learners. I met with Barbara and told her that I had been noticing more and more that she seemed unhappy here. We had a good discussion about how she had been feeling about her colleagues and work—whether she was right or was misguided in her thinking, those were her feelings— and I told her that my top goal for her was for her to be happy. I presented her with the letter of recommendation and told her that I'd never stand in the way of her happiness, and I want her to find a place to work that would make her happy. Barbara, to my surprise, was very accepting of this message. She took the letter and thanked me for my support. About a month later, during our summer vacation, Barbara contacted me to let me know she had accepted a job in a neighboring state and thanked me again for the letter of recommendation.

It benefitted Barbara to leave and take a fresh start, for her own mental health and happiness, and it ultimately benefitted my school that a constant source of anxiety for my staff was no longer present. It was also done kindly, as the letter of recommendation was a positive one.

For most teachers, where you work is a choice. Especially now in a crisis of teacher shortages nationwide, if a teacher isn't happy working at one school, they have the freedom to pursue another. We are all creatures of habit, so changing schools may seem impossible even when the fit is poor. Giving Barbara a simple "push" towards something else ended up being successful. If the people who *should* be leaving your school stay, the people who you need to stay might just get up and leave.

Improving the Teachers You Have

This chapter started with the hardest part—embracing discomfort and dealing with teachers who aren't a good fit. See *Dealing with Difficult Teachers* (Whitaker, 2014) for much more on this topic. Now let's turn to some strategies for improving the teachers we have, including addressing staff attendance, prioritizing professional learning, helping teachers help their students, and creating time to look at data.

Address Staff Attendance

We'll start with staff attendance, which is an issue at many schools. There are several ways that principals address this: one principal I knew began his time at a neighboring school by sitting down with each staff member, one on one, and handing them their last year's attendance to jumpstart a conversation about the importance of showing up. I can imagine this being very effective in some contexts, but I could also see things becoming combative if I, a new principal, held an inquisition against my entire staff.

There are also many principals who have informal conversations with staff who are often absent or tardy, in hopes of building relationships with that staff member first before putting them on the defensive. Every principal has a different style, and we each need to figure out what works best for us.

At a district administrator meeting I attended a few years back, the Chief of Human Resources shared the results of a district-wide teacher survey, sharing reasons why teacher attendance may be poor: one of the things shared as a top reason for teacher absenteeism is that there was "lack of motivation" for coming to work. One of my colleagues called out, "Isn't their paycheck motivation?" Others groaned. The Head of Human Resources stated that we needed to find ways to motivate our staffs to come to work. As you can imagine, this was met by some incredulous looks shared across the room and plenty of text messages being shot out amongst the principals:

"Now we're supposed to find fun reasons to motivate staff to come to work? Aren't the children their motivation?"

"If someone is abusing sick days, that should be dealt with by HR. I'm not here to sing and dance and coerce someone out of bed on a rainy day. It's their professional responsibility to show up."

"These teachers get 15 sick days a year; if they use them, they use them. What can I do, if contractually they get these days? Nothing we do is going to change anything."

And there it was again: *nothing we do will change anything.* That cannot be our mindset when looking to turn anything around. It's the easiest thing in the world to say and the hardest to get around. Turnaround leadership is also about trying different, outside-the-box ideas that you are going to bring inside your school. A fatalistic attitude simply wouldn't do. I was one of the people who rolled their eyes when the HR head was sharing her survey results. I, too, believed that people should only take sick days if they're really sick and should schedule appointments on their own time when possible. This is such an important job! I also knew that our poor attendance was not 100% attributed to serious, unavoidable illness. Our poor school attendance had been trending downward for years, and I felt it was attributed to the "big picture" of the state of our school. I knew there had to be a way to make people think twice before taking an "I'm tired" sick day, before taking an "it's raining" sick day, before taking a "had too much wine last night" sick day. That was the low-hanging fruit, and that was where I started. We can't control who is ill, but we can help shape the attitude that our staff have when they wake up on a school day. So here are a couple ideas to try.

1. Try New Methods of Absence Notification

Once I had pulled those three years of attendance data during my first summer as principal, I instituted a policy at our school that you must call, email, or text me to notify me that you will be absent. This was in addition to our district policy of entering your absence on a computer program electronically. This no-contact method of submitting a sick day was too easy; it's much easier to fib to your computer than it is to your principal. That extra step of having to contact me felt like an extra layer that removed a bit of the "anonymity" of rolling over and punching a few buttons on your cell phone the day after the Super Bowl.

2. Address Coverage Shortages

Our district, like so many, has an acute substitute shortage. In elementary schools, if a substitute teacher is not available, teachers have a pre-constructed "Split List" of where their students should be split up into other classrooms for the day. If a second-grade classroom has 25 students, that teacher submits a "Split List" to the office with the students split up into other classrooms for the day: five students into five different classrooms. Moreover, every teacher knows that writing substitute plans is often a larger task than actually coming into the building to work for a day! So a trend I had been noticing at my school among my most flagrantly absent teachers was that a teacher would call out just five minutes before the school day was set to begin, ensuring that there would be no substitutes available so late in the game. These teachers hadn't left any sub plans or sometimes didn't want to return the next day to a note detailing any issues or chaos that had ensued. They preferred knowing their students were split into the capable hands of their colleagues who, of course, had no say in the matter. What could I do to shine a light on this without ruffling too many feathers? I installed a large whiteboard in our main office which is updated each day with daily absences.

One side says "Coverage" and lists the staff member who is out with the name of their substitute. One side reads "No Coverage" and lists staff members who were out without any coverage. When a staff member called out at 8:51 (our day began at 8:55) I started to write the person's name, *and the time they called out.* Given the epidemic of late callouts, I thought this was fair play.

As staff members arrived at work to sign in, they'd take a look at the daily absence board and see which absences potentially affected their day. When people started noticing the "time of call-out" written next to certain names, it became clear that it was the same people calling out 5–10 minutes before the bell, all the time. All of a sudden, the board wasn't a jumble of names anymore; it was a pattern. If we had an average of 4–6 staff members out per day, it can be hard for busy, hardworking teachers to keep track of who is out and how often. They're not looking to be sick day detectives, they're only worried about their day-to-day smooth functioning of their classrooms! But when the time of the call-out was added, the "list of names" became a pattern. The names without a call-out time faded into the background, and the names with a time of call-out were remembered.

This helped staff see the "why" behind the late-in-the-game decision to split students and why students would arrive unprepared to their classrooms for the day. This opened a new door: teachers started to put the heat on each other, seeing that the cause of this additional stress was a small group of reoccurring sick day abusers, rather than simply losing a spin on the imaginary game show "What Will the Principal Do to Us Today?" I was showing, not telling—there was no need to run around and call people out; I didn't need to write an explicit memo warning of the district's sick day policy and touting the importance of good staff attendance. I added the time of the call-out on the white board, and it was game-changing.

I imagined teachers walking outside to pick up their classes at the 8:55 bell, having discussions somewhat like this:

> *Patty: Nina called out at 8:51 again. How did she not know she was sick until 4 minutes before the school day starts? She lives half an hour away! She had to know before 8:51.*
>
> *Marco: She knew she wasn't coming in. She wasn't prepared. She waited to call in. Now it's our problem.*
>
> *Patty: This is a pattern now. I may say something to her . . . it's really affecting my classroom to have five extra students*

every day, with no assignments. I'm taking time away from my first graders to support her students and find them some appropriate work.

I will never know if conversations such as this took place. But what I do know is that staff attendance improved exponentially when the message was sent that *someone is noticing, someone is paying attention.* My goal was not to create in-fighting amongst my staff members, but a colleague telling you to get it together and leave some sub plans can do significantly more than a top-down intervention.

Of course, I continued to document patterns of attendance and addressed my concerns directly with staff members who may have been abusing sick time. This strategy of adding the call-out time to the absence board was not in lieu of taking responsibility for documenting it. It was a pre-emptive strike; a strategy to hopefully eliminate the behavior before it required formal addressing.

Keep Professional Learning Front-of-Mind

Another way to improve the teachers you have is to make sure that professional learning is continual, not a one-time event. During my first year in the turnaround school, we participated in a three-part professional development series on the SIOP (Sheltered Instructional Observation Protocol) model in order to support our English Language Learners. This was something I had a great deal of experience in, so I was able to co-facilitate the professional development sessions with the district facilitators. It was a great kickoff to being an instructional leader at my school and was a good opportunity to present my staff with some strategies and scaffolds they could use to support the English Language Learners in their classrooms.

What happens after many after-school professional learning sessions? People arrive to work the next day, maybe taking a tip or two from the session, and resort back to their comfortable routines and ways of doing things. I felt that the strategies and components of the SIOP Model were so valuable, that I would revisit the strategies in my Weekly Bulletin and post pictures with captions when I saw a teacher or a classroom engaged in one of the activities we had discussed at our PD session. The goal here was to "make things stick." We had a long way to go in terms of our academic goals, and focusing on supporting our ELLs was a critical step. The strategies, lessons, and activities we learned about through SIOP training weren't specific to second language learners—they were just great teaching!

As leaders, we want to spread the good work being done and make sure people have ample exposure to the topics discussed at these after-school sessions. If we don't continue to keep this wonderful professional learning top-of-mind, then we'll be reinforcing the notion that "nothing sticks." In my case, this was good, valuable content. And unlike a new program or curricula where we're trained on how to utilize a resource, this was about the way we teach our students. This was about the way we deliver content, no matter the program or curriculum. This was professional development that would affect the way our students are able to receive and comprehend instruction. How do you ensure it doesn't "go away," like the latest reading program or the newest online fad that the district decides to cut funding for? Below are two strategies you can try, peer observation and Pineapple Charts.

1. Peer Observation

What's even more powerful than learning about teaching strategies? Seeing them in action. I began searching out what I wanted to see and getting teachers into the rooms where I found it happening. Unfortunately, it wasn't as easy as saying, "Hey everyone, Amanda is crushing it when she employs Reviewing Key Vocabulary into her lessons. I want to get the whole first grade team into her room, so you can learn from her!" Sound the screeching tires! Maryann would think, "Oh Amanda's been doing this for five years; I've been doing this for 20 years. What am I going to learn from a new teacher like that? I'm all set," or Christine may think, "Am I not doing a good enough job of reviewing Key Vocabulary? Oh my gosh—she doesn't think I'm doing it well."

The last thing I was trying to do by facilitating peer observations was pit staff members against each other or make anyone doubt themselves. I wanted to celebrate good teaching in the hope that teachers would adopt some great ideas and continue to grow and improve to the benefit of our students. We would get around this by letting all staff members know that we'd be spending their weekly hour of grade level planning participating in peer observations. Rather than take one grade level team into another member of the team's classroom, we would take the whole first grade team to observe in a kindergarten or a second-grade classroom. This way it didn't feel as if I was choosing a "best" room on the team. We'd spend the first half hour observing during a block of a reading or a math lesson, taking notes. The teacher who was being observed would know in advance, and we'd plan out exactly what the grade level team was hoping to observe. I'd be able to say to Amanda, "the last time I was in your room during your reading block, you did such a fantastic job reviewing Key Vocabulary with your students. I especially loved the way you used visuals and models. Would you mind if I bring the second-grade team into your classroom next week, at the same time, for a peer observation?"

We'd convene in the team room after the observation, sharing what we noticed and what we saw that we'd like to try. I would always conclude the session with the teachers making a chart titled "Something you did today that I'm going to try!" and have each team member contribute a thought and sign the chart, which I would present to Amanda. It was a meaningful token of thanks and went far in terms of building community.

2. Pineapple Charts

Another idea you can try is to create a Pineapple Chart. It is so named because the pineapple is the symbol of hospitality, and it's meant to more easily facilitate mutual observation among staff. Teachers could sign up on the chart for something they would like to share with colleagues. You can roll it out by asking teachers, is there something you're proud of, or something you feel you're doing well, that you would like to share with your colleagues? Teachers could list ideas on the Pineapple Chart. You also want teachers to be able to use it—if they are brave and vulnerable enough to do so—to sign up for things they'd like to see or learn more about.

In my school, we hung the Pineapple Chart up in the Teachers' Room, and the response was understandably slow at first. I pulled my leadership team of teachers aside and asked them if they could please kick this off. I requested that they each sign up for one thing they think other teachers may want to see in action, or one thing that they felt teachers could learn from them. We started to see the chart get filled in:

- ◆ *Miss Jackson, Room 216- IRLA one-on-one conferencing*
- ◆ *Mr. Haines, Room 116- Number Talks*
- ◆ *Mr. Klein, Room 118- Secret Stories phonics lessons*

Teachers would list the days/times they'd be doing these things, and if a teacher wanted to attend, all they had to do was email my Assistant Principal and me to request the time and we'd get them coverage. The list of requests soon grew, too. Most people wanted to learn more about online programs and software. Others wanted to observe programs they didn't use but may want to purchase for the future. Others wanted to see some classroom management strategies. Yes, yes, and yes!

- ◆ *Miss Washington- would like to learn more about Nearpod?*
- ◆ *Mr. Burns- would like to see a more effective end of the day dismissal procedure?*
- ◆ *Mrs. Smith- would like to learn more about Wilson's Fundations interventions?*

The difference between the strategic, pre-planned peer observations as a follow-up to staff professional development and the Pineapple Chart was that we tried to keep the Pineapple Chart as informal as possible. You can arrange for the coverage, or even cover the class yourself, but you can leave it up to the staff members to decide how they want to reflect, implement, and grow their professional relationships.

When teachers hear that there is a PD offering by the school, state, or district, they can sometimes roll their eyes and think

"Great, another boring PD I have to go to." Some PD is tedious, but others can genuinely change a classroom permanently. The Pineapple Chart makes PD a simple, casual thing that can be constantly happening throughout your school.

You can check in with the teachers during planning meetings: "How's the Pineapple Chart doing? Do you need anything else from me?" If it is empty, you can try to revive it. There is a bit of management required, but it doesn't need to be managed by you. You can delegate the Pineapple Chart to a teacher leader, who is even more in tune than you are as to how best it could be utilized.

By creating opportunities for teachers to observe others in action, you send the message that professional growth is important. Looping back to professional development from previous years sends the message that what was important last year has not been forgotten this year. That can be hard to do! The speed of new district and state initiatives can be dizzying. But if something is important enough that you asked your staff to stay after work to engage in the learning, you'll want to ensure that it doesn't just drift away.

Help Teachers Help Their Students

What are your pathways for students needing support? In my school, we realized we needed to create a quicker, easier pathway. Traditionally, teachers were asked to fill out lengthy and arduous district forms to refer a child. Some teachers, overwhelmed by the amount of paperwork, would not faithfully refer struggling students. This resulted in administration or academic coaches resorting to "punitive" measures such as mandating the process, monitoring student data, and documenting when teachers were out of compliance by not referring.

We felt that with the amount of need at our school—more than 80% of our students were below or significantly below grade level—it should not be so difficult for teachers to refer students for support. During my second year at the turnaround school, we created a simple "Wellness Team Referral Form" which was very user-friendly. Teachers would refer a student they were concerned about, indicate whether the concerns were academic, behavioral, or both, and submit to the Wellness Team, who receives the referral and directs the form to the staff members who would be most appropriate to "case manage" the referral.

Behavioral referrals would go directly to the School Psychologist or Social Worker, reading referrals would go directly to the Reading Coach, and so on.

We asked ourselves: what was more important, that teachers learned the process or that students received support? Once the goal of students quickly receiving support was established, we backmapped the most simple and efficient way for teachers to refer their students.

What is your process for student supports, and where could it possibly be streamlined? Remember that by lightening the load on our teachers, we can ensure that students always get exactly the support they needed.

Create Time to Examine Data

Again, it's beneficial for professional learning to be ongoing. Our district had in-house substitutes not only to cover daily absences but also to support experiences such as Deep Data Dives. We provided coverage for our teachers so we could extend their weekly one-hour grade level planning time to 90 minutes or two hours once every quarter.

Administrators, Instructional Coaches, and grade level teams examine benchmark data, progress monitoring data, and interim assessment data. We compare this data to the reports we get from our reading and math curricular assessments, data from our online intervention platforms, and other measures. This time is used to reevaluate small groupings, draft walk-to-read possibilities, and concludes with an updated "to do list" of students in need of additional supports, such as Teacher Support Team referral. Doing this "with" teachers and not just assigning it "to" teachers creates a collaborative culture and reinforces the idea that these are *our* students. This approach still holds teachers accountable but places the high expectations on the team.

Final Thoughts

Leaders of turnaround schools grapple with letting teachers go, and improving the ones we have. Letting teachers go can be tricky and time consuming, whether you're documenting extreme cases, dealing with the "quit but stayed" staff, or giving people a gentle push. But doing so is important for the culture of the school, for your best teachers who may not be getting your attention—and more importantly, for your students! Improving the teachers you have can be done through peer observation, Pineapple Charts, data dives, and other methods that make the learning stick, and that hold teachers accountable and with high expectations.

6

Coaching Teachers to Handle Student Behavior

The goal when a student acts out in class is to de-escalate with the student and place an emphasis on preventing the behavior from happening again in the future. Yet in some cases, teachers are happy when a student is removed from the classroom, then visibly and audibly disappointed when they return.

As principals, each behavior call we receive can feel like being in the game of Whack-A-Mole. I remember I'd receive an office call that a second grader was hiding in the closet, noncompliant and refusing to come out. As I was darting up to that classroom, I'd receive another walkie call that a fight broke out in the fifth-grade wing. I'd reverse course—Kevin would have to sit in the closet for a few more minutes—and run toward the fight. This pattern feels like it will never end.

But as we discussed earlier in the book, when there's an issue with the students, look at the adults first. Next year the students may be different but it doesn't mean anything if the adults stay the same. In my case, *it was the culture of the building* that needed the attention and the work. It would take time to leverage leadership and build up staff in the school who can take the lead on situations such as Kevin in the closet. There needs to be protocols for things such as what to do when children cannot attend a field trip due to parent non-consent. There was so much need for structural change, amidst the constant demands of the day-to-day.

DOI: 10.4324/9781003321323-9

Of course, we don't want teachers to think, "She's just another principal who doesn't support us." But we know that support does not equal regularly taking the children who cause distractions out of your classroom and sitting them in a holding space. Support does not equal sending the child home every time they're dealing with complicated emotions. We know this because we have seen it happen in so many schools. These actions may placate the teachers in the moment, but what have we done for our students in need of real support? And what have we done to increase the skills of the adults in our school?

Behavior is a form of communication, and rather than ignoring the issue—*go play Roblox in my office so Mrs. Lawrence can teach math*—we need to get better at identifying the root causes of children's emotional outbursts, so we can address the actual issues. This will, in turn, eventually lead to getting these children back in class and learning. In many cases, we need to determine what constitutes a referral: which behaviors should be managed in the classroom by the teacher, and which behaviors should be raised to building administration for additional supports?

In my school, I felt strongly that if we were to remove a student from class whose antisocial behaviors indicated a desire to be removed, we would be reinforcing these negative behaviors by rewarding them. What you feed grows. We'd essentially be saying, "Yes, Duane, since you threw that chair, you get to play on the computer all day, or go home with Mom so you can play your video games all day." And what does that teach Duane's friend Steven, who is also academically struggling and gets frustrated during math class? Act out, and it's a ticket out of here . . . what a relief that must be!

Creating Protocols for Handling Behavior

Those first few years, my psychologist, social worker, new Assistant Principal, and I did a lot of work on the processes that would be followed when we received an office call due to a student behavior or safety concern. We delivered Professional Development on Tier 1 classroom managed behaviors, and strategies to support students in the classroom. We created protocols for communication between Wellness Team Staff and the Classroom Teacher, so that the teacher would 1) be aware that the student was returning to class and 2) be better equipped to welcome that child back into class. That second part would be a heavier lift, as it includes a complete change in mindset. We needed to create clear guidelines as to what constituted an office call, and what should be handled in the classroom—we'd refer to certain minor behaviors as "classroom-managed behaviors." We had to break the habit of teachers calling the principal for students calling out across the room or getting out of their seats without permission. Those occurrences can definitely annoy a teacher who is trying to teach a lesson but can and should be addressed by the teacher.

One of the biggest issues we had to grapple with was the delicate balance between honoring a teacher's feelings when they call the office due to fear, panic, or frustration, and supporting the student's right to an education by not pulling them out of the classroom so much. It's important to remember that the student writing on the bathroom stall door doesn't deserve more of your attention than the 24 other students who are engaged and ready to learn. If we wanted to move our school out of corrective action status with the state, we had to ensure that the students' opportunity to learn wasn't being chipped away at on a daily basis. So what was the solution?

Each day, our team would jump back on that hamster wheel and respond to behavior calls, work with students on therapeutic or restorative solutions, call parents in, and even suspend when necessary with the short- or long-term goal of returning a calmer, ready-to-learn student to the classroom. Still, we were observing that some staff members were not implementing any Tier 1 behavior management systems, and those staff would be the loudest critics when minor, annoying behaviors would repeat, and the child was still arriving to school every day and entering that classroom.

When I learned of the griping and criticizing that "nothing was done," I'd think, "Wow, what do they want? Would they like me to catapult this child into space so that the problem just magically disappears? What do they want me to do?" Then it dawned on me—just *ask them*. So I tweaked the forms to get on the same page. Here are some ways you can consider changes to your own referral processes.

Revamping Behavior Referral Forms

Behavior Referrals are often a long-simmering source of frustration. Overhauling the form can help you get on the same page as your staff—and vice versa.

Early on, when we began this journey of transformation, we found it was very common for people to criticize the way that building administration responded to office behavior calls or written behavior referrals. It often felt that the way administration "disciplined" a child, either through conferencing, reflection, or a meeting with parents, was not the outcome that the classroom teacher had hoped for. This disappointment, however, was rarely transmitted directly to me. Instead, it took the form of gossip, whispers, and resentments—acid rain for any school's morale. This building-wide culture of feeling a lack of support with student behaviors had started years ago. No matter how I handled a disrespectful outburst, an elopement, a fight—unless I exiled that student, the critics were not going to be satisfied. There were constant mutterings of things such as "Nothing ever happens to Xavier!" or "I never get any support" that had become taglines. There was a lot of work on mindset, proactive classroom management, and de-escalation strategies ahead of us.

In these cases, it can be effective to ask staff what they want. So on the behavior referral form, which includes sections such as "location of incident" and "describe the behavior," I added a section at the bottom that says *What is your ideal outcome in how building administration handles this situation?* It was so simple, yet such a huge game changer at my school. Teachers weren't sure what to put there at first. Even the top complainers were hesitant to put in writing "Suspension!" when the forms were first distributed. They also couldn't bring themselves to say "just take him out of my room" because that is overtly denying a child his right to an education. **When we asked them to partner with us to determine a sensible response to this child's behavior, the critics grew quieter.**

Through the work we did, most teachers knew that not every minor annoyance would qualify for a day of missed instruction. They also knew deep down that many times a student's behavior was motivated by wanting to be sent home. Home is where their family is; home is where their video games are; home is comforting where school is challenging. We did not want to feed into this pattern, as it would encourage the behavior to continue. This was a lightbulb moment for many.

How could we reverse this cycle of teachers versus administrators if we didn't do something differently? This doesn't mean that whatever the teacher suggested on the behavior referral was greenlit. I wasn't going to suspend a child for a week for refusal to line up for Art class just because the teacher's patience was running out. The goal was instead that we would try to accommodate the teacher and support them in their daily frustrations with behaviors by learning what that teacher thought would be an appropriate way to handle it. And *that* was eye opening. I really did get inside their heads, which allowed me to diagnose where the situation had gone awry and where the attention was needed.

Some teachers were insightful and reasonable, albeit brutally honest, in that section: "I want this child to get counseling," "I want this child to have a meeting with his parents and the principal to discuss the severity of these actions," etc. . . . Some were unreasonable: "I want this child transferred to another school because he has ruined his relationship with every student in my classroom" simply for being disruptive. What I learned here was that our entire staff, myself included, needed to dig deeper in identifying root causes of behavior.

If we spend the majority of our time punishing, removing, and focusing on consequences, we aren't focused on prevention and repair. The best teachers focus on repair and prevention. They aren't looking for a "public bloodletting." They want to move forward with the behaviors not happening again and see improved behavior and student success.

The changes to this form made it crystal clear which teachers were focused on prevention and which were focused on punishment. Of course, there are times consequences were appropriate, times when we needed to suspend. But by bringing the teachers in to the decision-making process, we really did start to eliminate the mindless gripes in the teacher's lounge. This section caused teachers to think about the situation and come up with an appropriate solution first before handing the situation to me. If a teacher's suggestion was outrageous, I had an opening to have an honest conversation with that teacher about classroom management and appropriate consequences. It also created an opportunity for me to tailor professional development to my teachers based on need. If I had a group of teachers writing children up for behavior that could have been proactively avoided with tighter procedures and routines, this was data for *me*. I knew we needed more professional development on this very topic. What are your goals for behavior referrals, and how can you change your process to reflect those goals?

Coaching Teachers to Handle Difficult Situations

One example of how I used the new behavior referral form to 1) conference, 2) coach, and 3) support a teacher was in the case of Ms. Carter. Ms. Carter had made a name for herself as being extremely negative, toxic, and anti-administration. It wouldn't have mattered if I were younger or older, male or female, new to education or a crusty veteran: Ms. Carter was against anything I had to say before she even met me.

Ms. Carter was growing more and more agitated with a student named Jasmine who was acting out of character as the year progressed. I received many referrals from Ms. Carter that said Jasmine had been bothering some of the girls in her classroom all day. Jasmine had been poking one girl in particular while they walked to the lunchroom or the bathrooms; she had been out of her seat causing drama in the classroom during independent work; she had been arguing with the girls incessantly about all sorts of topics. I'd read these referrals and think, *What is going on in this classroom? How are we getting this deep into dramatic conversations when instruction should be happening?* This same teacher would very vocally tell her peers in the staff lounge, "Every day Jasmine thinks she runs the room. And our principal isn't going to suspend her. I get no support!"

In the section of the form that asks what the ideal outcome would be for how building administration handles the situation, Ms. Carter wrote, "in-house suspension when she starts to bother the other girls." This told me that Ms. Carter wants this child out. She wants removal.

Remembering to treat all employees as if they are good (Whitaker, 2020), I decided to request a meeting with Ms. Carter to discuss how we should move forward to support Jasmine, and I approached her by assuming she had already done her due diligence. When we met, I asked her three questions:

◆ *What is your expectation for students not in your reading group, during small group instruction?*
◆ *Can I see a copy of your line order so we can make some strategic moves together?*
◆ *What did Jasmine's parents say when you told them how concerned you are about her recent classroom behaviors?*

Spoiler alert: Ms. Carter didn't have a line order, and she felt that "they're in fourth grade, so they should know what to do when I'm working with another group!" No expectations for independent work time had been explicitly taught, which meant there was no opportunity to reward or reinforce when students were following or not following those expectations. The conditions to proactively avoid unnecessary drama did not exist in her classroom. Most importantly, Ms. Carter had not yet reached out to Jasmine's family to troubleshoot and learn if something was going on in Jasmine's life. And when I say "yet," I'm being hopeful, because I'm not sure that phone call was ever going to be made.

Principals' jobs are to coach, but Ms. Carter made this a particular challenge. She was a veteran teacher who knew that classroom management was an imperative part of teaching fourth grade. Was she being lazy and choosing to just complain about Jasmine, or did she truly need a refresher on how this all works? Whatever the real problem was, we were able to have the discussion that removing Jasmine from her educational environment without ever touching base with her parents did not make sense. I was able to set up a meeting with Jasmine's parents and Ms. Carter, and I made sure I attended.

We learned in this meeting that Jasmine's father had just lost his job and the family lost their apartment. They were a family of four, and were staying at Jasmine's grandmother's apartment, staying in the living room while they figured out their next steps. Due to the move, they had to give their dog away because the grandmother's apartment doesn't allow pets. That had been tough for Jasmine. I watched Ms. Carter's face intently as she listened to Jasmine's family explain that they have seen her act out at home, and how they didn't even realize this was affecting her at school, too. Jasmine's parents were apologetic and embarrassed. We offered to connect them with Family Services in an effort to help the family get back on their feet.

Upon reflection, the only person in this story who had any right to be complaining about a "lack of support" was Jasmine. Her teacher had been hoping for her to be removed from the classroom, rather than setting up any sort of proactive system or having any sort of conference with Jasmine or her parents to prevent future behaviors or seek to support.

Behavior is a form of communication. Listen to it!

When You Really Need to Intervene

Sometimes coaching teachers isn't enough, and you do need to step in. My first year as an administrator, I was an Assistant Principal. I was brand new to the school and working under a very popular, established principal. She and I were walking through the building, and we passed by a teacher who had pulled a student into the hallway and was scolding him. Her tone of voice was extremely sharp. She was standing right in front of him, causing him to have to look up at her, while she loudly and harshly upbraided him for something that I assume had just transpired in the classroom. I remember thinking, *Yikes, she seems tough*. I wondered if this was always how she spoke to children.

We kept walking. A few minutes later, the principal asked me, "What will you do when the student's mother calls the school later this afternoon, wanting to know more information about why her son was yelled at?" I paused for a moment, trying to understand not only the question but the event itself: we had both walked by without figuring out what had been going on. As I thought about an answer, this experienced principal told me something that I have never forgotten, and that I have carried with me throughout every interaction and every building walk I have done as principal. She said, "As a principal, everything that happens in this school is your business." Talk about a powerful realization.

Often, the most uncomfortable moments are precisely the ones in which you need to intervene the most. The goal is not to overpower a teacher or take their power away when disciplining students, but to learn what is happening in your building, in an effort to continue, grow, or eliminate the behaviors. And when something is unacceptable, have the confidence to step in and redirect. "I'll take it from here, Ms. Andrews" is a personal favorite of mine; it lets the adult know that you would prefer to take over while not addressing what you're displeased with in front of the child (and ultimately, tempering that teacher's authority for future management).

You might be thinking, "But I am the new person! I am still getting to know everyone! It was their house; I'm just learning everyone and trying to figure out how to do my job well. That's just how they do things here." Remember that everything in the school is your business. And if they know you are aware of it, they know you accept it (Whitaker, 2020). It might be hard to keep up the pace, but it's important to address the things you see happening.

Tougher is when you *don't* see something, only to later find out it's happening under your nose. This can be a recurring problem no matter how much progress we've made in school transformation. One particularly illustrative example: Well into the school year, I learned that a second-grade teacher was withholding Music and Art class from any students who didn't complete assignments from the morning. Moreover, these "morning work" assignments were nothing more than busy work that had been assigned while the teacher was taking attendance or working with a small group. If I had been one of those students, I'm not sure I would've been motivated to do them either.

Stacey was an outspoken, often-negative teacher who was notorious for yelling both at her students and her colleagues. I learned that Stacey was dropping students off at her coworkers' doors on her class's way to Music or Art, saying loudly for all to hear: "She's not going to Music today, she didn't finish her morning assignment. Can I put her with you?" and the other teachers—out of fear of Stacey—would just take the child. This was happening at least once a week with every student who didn't complete an assignment from that morning. When a teacher, Kris, finally got up the courage to inform me that this was happening, she also asked me not to let Stacey know I heard this from her.

It was a phenomenon I quickly got used to: people reaching out for help, due to a student being mistreated or a teacher behaving inappropriately, and then asking me to keep it a secret. Should everyone's fear of Stacey rule over what's best for children? (HINT: The answer to that question is never, ever "yes.") But, building trust with teachers who've come to share something with me is important. All leaders should aspire to have teachers who know that the right thing to do when children are being mistreated is to address it with a person who can help, rather than just seeing it and accepting it.

If I broke Kris's trust and marched into Stacey's room announcing, *This is going to stop! I know about Music class being withheld!* it would then send Stacey straight into Kris's classroom to argue with her that she shouldn't have told the principal, she knows better since she's a veteran teacher, and so on. That heated exchange would exacerbate the negative school culture that already existed. Kris would then likely try to smooth things over with Stacey and would most certainly not trust me with information like this again. Who wins here? Certainly not me, and definitely not the students. Additionally other teachers would know that the teacher who finally had the nerve to tell the principal what had happened ended up getting the brunt of the other teacher's ire. One or two instances like this and all communication with the school leader will be eliminated.

My other option was to stake out Stacey's classroom each week right around Music or Art time, watching for which students she was dropping off and keeping from Music class. Then, I could make up a reason for popping into the Music room looking for one of those students. I could feign surprise at not finding the student and ask Stacey, *Where's Keisha? She's marked present, but she's not with the class! The Music teacher has not seen her. Do we need to do an all-call? Should we call the police due to a missing child?* This plan seems perfectly doable, what with all the extra time for stakeouts and role playing that administers have built into their days.

But I did do that. You bet I did! Stacey was part of the problem at my school in terms of the way we treat children: asserting power over her students by withholding one period per week that many of our students really look forward to. My approach was calm: *Stacey, Where's Keisha?* When Stacey answered me with a location, I was able to ask why. *Why is Keisha doing a phonics worksheet with Miss Summers instead of participating in Music class with her classmates?* When Stacey told me what she deemed to be a perfectly reasonable answer—*Keisha was too busy talking this morning and didn't finish her phonics worksheet*—I was able to have a conversation with Stacey about better ways to approach work completion and manage behavior in the classroom. Attending Music class was a right, not a privilege. Additionally, if Stacey was this worried about Keisha's academic achievement being affected by this low rate of ditto completion, why wasn't Stacey pulling her aside, during class time or planning period, to intervene? In a school where people have gotten used to the way things are, it might have been years since someone asked Stacey these questions—questions she desperately needed to hear.

Documenting Your Discipline Discussions

The conversation with Stacey needed to be documented. I'm not suggesting that every single conversation you have with any member of your staff that needs redirecting should go through a formal process, but I'm warning that conversations that happen "on the fly" will exist only in your memory from that point forward.

The goal of these conversations is ultimately *changed behavior moving forward*. And sometimes an off-the-cuff conversation is all a person needs to correct a behavior. But if this behavior remains a habit or doesn't change, you'll need to move forward with documentation. If the only proof you have that Stacey has been withholding arts education from her students is memories of the times you've talked, you're starting the progressive discipline ladder from scratch.

Sometimes documentation can just be a supportive email framed as a "thank you." It needn't always be on formal district letterhead, memorializing a directive or naming a reprimand. Here's an example of what I might have emailed Stacey that afternoon, after dismissal:

> *Stacey, Thank you for taking the time to meet with me on your planning period this morning. I appreciated our conversation and share your concerns about Keisha's lack of growth in reading.*
>
> *Just to recap: You are working on a referral to the Teacher Support Team to obtain some Tier 2 supports and strategies for Keisha in phonics and fluency. Please let me know if the TST is unable to schedule this meeting for you within the next two weeks.*
>
> *Thank you for understanding that we cannot withhold Arts education classes such as Music and Art in an effort to support work completion in other subject areas. If you need additional support with Keisha moving forward, please always feel free to reach out.*

We should always treat everybody like our best people (Whitaker, 2020). Believe it or not, you can handle these situations while still treating teachers this way. I asked where Keisha was and allowed that to lead us into a conversation that needed to be had. No students deserve to be missing out on Arts education every week as a punishment.

Also make sure that the situation *lives somewhere*, even in an informal email such as the example on the previous page. If Stacey continued to withhold Art, or Music, or recess from her students because they did not complete a morning worksheet, I'd have a date-stamped email proving that I had already addressed the situation; now we had a pattern. This would enable me to move up the ladder of Progressive Discipline and address it more forcefully in the future, if need be.

Insert yourself. Somewhere in your building, Keisha will be glad that you did.

Final Thoughts

When turning around a school, you might get called regularly to help handle student behavior issues. Improving your behavior referral system, with teacher input, can bring about positive changes. Coach teachers on how to deal with difficult behavior so you don't always have to intervene . . . but also know when you *do* need to get involved. Our main goal is to protect our students, not our teachers. And remember, sometimes the difficult behavior is the students. And sometimes it is the adults.

7

Implementing Tight and Logical Instructional Time

In schools with low achievement data, it is important to get a handle on instructional and data analysis as soon as possible. Ask yourself: what is our school's biggest barrier to student success? Right away, you may think of several factors, generally a mix of things within and outside your school's walls. Pose the question again, but with an addendum: what is our school's biggest barrier to student success *that is within our control?* We can't eliminate poverty, trauma, and family strife, but we can work to support students who are experiencing these things. What we *can* do is improve instructional practice, lesson efficacy, during- and after-school activities, and the experience our children have when they step into our care each day.

Start with Instructional Learning Walks

During my first year at the turnaround school, I would often go on building walks. Sometimes I'd go alone, sometimes with our reading coach, and other times with district administrators. Far too often, we'd go on an "Instructional Learning Walk" and wouldn't actually see any instruction.

DOI: 10.4324/9781003321323-10

We wouldn't see any instruction. Let that sink in. Now, that doesn't mean that instruction wasn't happening at our school! It did mean that almost every time I did an instructional walk, I wouldn't witness any behaviors I could provide real feedback on. I'd see students working independently, students in transition ("Oh hi! We were just lining up for the bathrooms!"), students on the rug listening to a story, or students on devices while a teacher was collecting fluency data one-on-one. I'd leave classrooms feeling uncertain what to do with what I had just observed. Where was the core, grade-level instruction? Why do I have such bad luck that I continue to enter classrooms as they were "just coming to the rug to hear a story!" or "just lining up to go to the bathroom"?

Some days, I'd walk the halls and see three or four classrooms lined up to use the bathrooms at the same time, in addition to having another classroom attempt to walk down the hall as they were passing to Music class or Lunch. The hallways were crowded, inviting student behavioral issues. How much instructional time was being lost here?

The truth was that although there were a good number of classrooms that were engaged in meaningful, tier one instruction, there was also a culture in this building that focused more on "managing" the children than teaching them. This meant either putting them on an online activity while the teacher read with students one-on-one, or giving students "busy work" while the teacher facilitated small group instruction. And that was in my "mediocre" to "good" classrooms! The poorer teachers were struggling so badly to manage behaviors—or, in many instances, creating chaotic classroom environments where behaviors grew and thrived—that it was hard to tell exactly what was going on at any given time.

For me to enter *those* classrooms and be able to collect authentic data, I had to eliminate the "we were just transitioning to the rug to hear a story!" and "We were just lining up for the bathroom, sorry!" from happening each time I entered the room. Though this was sometimes happening authentically to be sure, I had the gut feeling that it was also sometimes happening strictly because the principal had just entered the classroom with an iPad, ready to observe instruction.

Flesh Out the Schedules

We already had individual teacher schedules that teachers received at the start of each school year, delineating where in each day the class would engage in Literacy, Science, Math, Art, Lunch, and so on. We had instructional minutes to meet, and these schedules served as a guide for teachers when starting the school year. My instructional coaches and I decided to give teachers the opportunity to really flesh out their schedules and be able to note exactly what portion of the literacy block or math block was happening at exactly which times. We'd take these block schedules and, during the first weeks of school, work as grade level teams to flesh out detailed, more specific schedules that delineated particular components of their instructional blocks.

For example, a typical fourth-grade schedule on a Monday morning at my school may look something like this:

Time	Monday
9:25-9:30	ARRIVAL
9:30-10:00	SOCIAL STUDIES
10:00-10:30	PE
10:30-11:00	ELA
11:00-11:30	ELA
11:30-12:00	ELA
12:00-12:30	SCIENCE
12:30-1:00	LUNCH

With schedules as vague as this, I could walk in this classroom door at most times of the day and be unsure of what I should see. We moved toward tightening up schedules with more specific blocks of time. ELA in this classroom would still occur from 10:30–12:00, but the updated schedules called out the specific components of the literacy block that our district curriculum required. For example, the same fourth grade teacher would work with me, my instructional coach, and his fourth-grade team to edit the original schedule to look more like this:

10:05–10:30 Foundational Skills
-SEL, Morning Circle
-Foundational Skills (~15min)

10:30–11:00 Read, Write, & Discuss Complex Texts
- ARC Lesson
-Read-Aloud

11:00–11:20 Writers' Workshop
-Mini-lesson
-Conferencing
-Small group instruction

11:20–12:00 Readers' Workshop (RW2-Independent Reading)
-Power Goal Groups
-1:1 Conferencing (IRLA/Level Setting)
-Independent Reading with a Purpose
-Stations/Centers
-iRead MyPath (60 min per week)

12:00–12:10: Bathroom Break

12:10–12:35 English Language Development
-Vista connect (MLL Students)
- Math Just-in-time supports & Power Goal activities (non-MLL Students)

12:40–1:30 LUNCH/RECESS

Instructional minutes are paramount, and we should not be losing 20 minutes of instruction a day with two whole-class bathroom breaks. We established with teachers that the expectation is not to take the entire 10 minutes; it's to utilize a few minutes *within that 10-minute window.*

We put out a whole-school schedule: We have one restroom area on the first floor and one on the second floor. That's not ideal for about 500 students, but it's what we have! Each classroom was assigned a 10-minute period for using the restrooms in the morning, and another block in the afternoon. The most important part that I felt was critical to include was that no classes should be using the bathroom during "passage time." That meant, on the hour or half hour, as classes are traveling to and from Art or PE, Music or Library, or Lunch. We didn't want to add to the crowd by having an entire class lined up in the halls, using the bathrooms.

What the bathroom schedule did, besides initially causing some grumbling, was eliminate the possibility that learning walks would consist of having the "bad luck" of entering classrooms *just as they were about to line up for the bathrooms*, every time. And it also supported students by maximizing their instructional minutes. No longer would a class arrive at the bathrooms, only to realize they were third in line, and have to stand respectfully and quietly for about 15 minutes as they wait for the two classrooms before theirs to finish up.

Though I was adamant about this change, I didn't want to thoughtlessly burden my teachers without consulting them first. I asked the team leaders: what do you think about having a time of day assigned to you, where you know the bathroom will be all yours, no hallway traffic? Each one I asked was enthusiastic: Christine shared that it's tougher to keep her class following hallway expectations when Mrs. F's class is there, too. Mrs. F had a loose grip on her students, putting it kindly. Patty thought the schedule sounded great because "it'll go quicker if we don't have to wait" and she could get back to teaching.

With their feedback, I was confident that this would be universally beneficial. The schedule honors my best teachers—those who didn't *need* a scheduled break because they were always teaching when I did an instructional walk—by ensuring that each class had a sacred time for this purpose every day during which they could take their class to the restrooms quickly and get right back to teaching. These teachers could then create their detailed schedules around their assigned bathroom times. Conversely, it created some structure for my other teachers who were more or less "winging it" each day, who struggled to plan effectively for efficient transitions and struggled to fit all components of the literacy or math blocks into their day. Now that these teachers have a consistent time of day for the bathroom break, I could support them better.

It also provided much-needed structure for the building as a whole. Teachers could walk their students back from the cafeteria without having to squeeze by several classes waiting for the bathroom. This removed the opportunity for issues to present themselves. No more, or at least much fewer, instances of "He banged into me!" or "That girl from my bus just stuck out her tongue at me!" as children passed in the hallway.

Bathroom schedules may reek of micromanagement to some, and that's okay. Every building is different and has different needs. If hallway passage does not affect other portions of your day, then don't feel a need to fix what isn't broken. At my school, I was experiencing a lot of bad habits that lingered from years of inconsistent leadership. I was having to manage behaviors all day, which was eating away at my ability to be an instructional leader. Little tweaks and changes such as the bathroom schedule announced that we'd be doing things differently. Doing the same thing over and over again but expecting different results— isn't that the definition of insanity? We decided to approach things differently, and it made a huge difference: hallways were calmer, transitions were quicker, and I was able to get into classrooms and collect data on instruction, not on transitions. I used the teachers' specific schedules to map out my instructional learning walks to ensure I would be present during core or small group instruction. This allowed us—allowed *me*—to get down to business.

Teachers can't control if a child will be in crisis or processing some "big feelings" during his ELA block on a Tuesday morning. You can't control if someone will pull the fire alarm, thus evacuating the entire school during the one hour on a Thursday that you had set aside for an instructional learning walk. There will always be a need for flexibility and pivoting in these professions, but you can't continue on the hamster wheel of allowing things that are fully within your control to dictate your school's success. It's important to control the controllables.

The same ideas apply at a secondary level. Is passing time between classes of the appropriate length? Do they need 6 minutes five times a day or will 4 minutes during each break suffice? How do teachers set the tone to immediately move into a learning environment when class time begins? Also, if teachers go into peers' classrooms to observe, don't feel the need for math to go into math only. Observing different subjects/grades can be equally valuable as you are really wanting them to see effective practices which are most often quite universal.

Always Attach Your Why

When I rolled out the bathroom schedule, I made sure to attach a "why." Attaching a "why" to all forms of communication, written and verbal, is a good habit to get into as much as possible. It is one of my communication non-negotiables. At a faculty meeting, I shared data from behavior write-up forms about the amount of incidents happening in the bathrooms, and then shared my anecdote about having the "worst luck" when it came to observing teachers right as they were lining up for the bathroom. I made it about them. I framed it as giving teachers their time back, so that they can focus more on instruction and less on waiting in the hallway.

When I sent the digital copies of the Bathroom Break schedule to my staff, it was attached to an email that highlighted the benefits:

- ◆ This minimizes wasted instructional time.
- ◆ This maximizes students' opportunities to learn.
- ◆ This decreases the amount of traffic in our hallways during main passage times, thus eliminating opportunities for chaos and disorder.

I started to get into the habit of attaching a "why" to everything. Here is another example: Every school in our state is required to publish a School Improvement Plan (SIP), and there are traditionally three overarching goals for improvement in this plan: a literacy goal, a math goal, and a student attendance goal. Teachers were expected to be familiar with the SIP. Technically, every single thing we do during the day should go towards improving student achievement, and the strategies outlined in that plan should be driving our instructional practices.

To streamline our efforts, every time we'd hold a meeting or planning session, I would note the SIP goal that the meeting was supporting right on the agenda. For example, if my Reading Coach was facilitating a grade-level planning time one week that focused on student writing strategies, we'd note "SIP Goals

1.1 & 1.2" at the bottom of the agenda. This outright eliminated comments such as "why are we doing this?" that so often accompany important meetings.

Oftentimes, plans like these are written by the leadership team—the principal, instructional coaches, district support staff—and are then seemingly "owned" by those same people. I wanted every teacher in our school to be able to own the goals and strategies themselves. It always felt like the coaches or principal would refer to the school improvement plan, and teachers knew what it was but couldn't tell you anything specific about it. By setting a precedent of framing meetings in terms of goals, our entire staff could now see the end goal of everything we did.

Attaching a "why" also helps bolster whole-school procedures and routines. In an effort to build a safer and more orderly environment, I directed all classes who were lining up after recess to re-enter the building via "Door 6." Some teachers balked at this: "But Door 4 is so much closer to my classroom!" and they were right, Door 4 *was* much closer to their classrooms. But what they didn't realize was that if they entered the school via Door 4 at the time their recess period ended, they'd be walking through a mass of classrooms that were passing to lunch at that time. Chaos and confusion would likely ensue, making it more difficult to ensure that all children stayed in line and entered the building in a respectful manner.

When I showed this new traffic pattern to the staff, I presented it with a map of the building, schoolyard, and lunchroom. I demonstrated that by entering via Door 6, they'd be walking with the flow of traffic and would have the whole hallway to themselves, as the classrooms passing to lunch would be moving away from their point of entry. When teachers saw the "why" behind the new procedure, it made sense to them too. This parlays into less pushback and a greater sense of cohesion than top-down edicts with no explanation.

Consider where you can attach a "why" to your own communications about routines or instructional practices. And best of all, the "why" should not be reserved for administrative staff. Whenever teachers approach you with a suggestion, ask them to outline *why* they have thought of this particular idea and why it would improve things.

Final Thoughts

How can you tighten up schedules, passing time, and hallway procedures so valuable instructional time isn't lost? How are you using your instructional walks to best help your teachers? Whether you need to improve the bathroom break procedure or something else, look at what needs to be tightened and where time can be used more effectively. You can't control everything related to learning and instruction, but you can control the controllables. And when you do, always be sure to attach the "why." Though some teachers may balk at the "why," remember that the most effective teachers ask themselves that question with everything they do. It is not adding to the load of your most effective staff members, it is just refining the practice among everyone else.

III

Influencing School Culture

8

Communicating Before You Need To

Communication—or, more often, a lack thereof—is one of the most common areas needing improvement in struggling schools. Climate and culture, key elements of school amelioration in themselves, tend to stem directly from how well communication is taking place. Instructional support and operational support also both depend heavily on communication. Being proactive sets the tone. When communicating important information or messaging, I try to be proactive with "pre-communication."

For example, you can include many forms of regular communication in your Weekly Bulletin, such as upcoming events or showcasing staff behaviors that you expect (*"Thank you Mr. Parsons for greeting students at the door as they enter the gym! Check out Rashidi's smile as he high-fives his PE teacher!"* as a caption for a picture in our Weekly Bulletin), highlighting to all staff the reason why we are here: the kids! This sort of communication is ongoing, it drives the vision, it updates staff on where we are in multiple areas of our school, and it sets the tone for further improvement.

Let's take a closer look at communicating for specific events, follow-ups after the fact, weekly communications, and more. And don't forget to proofread!

DOI: 10.4324/9781003321323-12

Communicating Specific Events: Details Matter

When communicating a specific event or activity (All-School Assembly, Reading Week, State Testing logistics), I try to be as detailed as possible to avoid any misunderstandings. One example of this is when working on a Coverage memo. Coverage—when one staff member has to take temporary responsibility for a colleague's responsibility—is the new groan-inducing buzzword in education these days, but it's always been a complicated puzzle.

Say your school has to move a few things around to accommodate teachers attending an in-school professional development workshop. You may be assigning some support staff to cover in classrooms. If I need the school Librarian to cover in a fourth grade classroom from 11:00–11:30, I can easily state that on my memo. But what is easy to miss—and will definitely be missed—is when that fourth grade class has Art just prior, from 10:30–11:00. Our fourth grade teacher is going to be at a professional development workshop and the Librarian, who is not necessarily privy to the whole-school schedule I'm using to write this coverage memo, will likely just report to that fourth grade classroom at 11:00 and not know that she is needed to first pick the children up from the Art room.

What happens then? This fourth grade class is waiting for the Librarian (who, bless her heart, has no idea she should be at the Art room) and the Art teacher is stuck waiting with the fourth grade class, all while the next class is impatiently waiting in the hallway. Things like this can aggravate staff members and cause complaining, which as you know can further contribute to negative culture and climate. We'll never eliminate complaining, and we'll never be able to fully manage people being on time. *But we can do everything in our power to eliminate the confusion*. In this particular coverage memo, I would write:

Coverage Today:

11:00–11:30, Room 207-Librarian Hannah

(Mrs. Hannah to pick up Room 207 from Art at 11:00 and take to the classroom. Coverage lasts until 11:30 at which time Teacher Mr. Connor will return to Room 207 from his professional development session.)

It's wordier, yes. But it eliminates the Librarian reporting to her coverage assignment to find an empty room, and then having to call the office and ask the already-busy secretary *where is Room 207?* The secretary will then need to look up the class's schedule, which takes time, all the while mayhem is breaking out in the Art room as the Art teacher is struggling to supervise two classes at once. He may also be trying to call the office, looking for Librarian Hannah. I'm exhausted just explaining it.

The "After Party" Email—Communicate After an Event, Too!

In many cases, you might also want to send an email after an event. I call them the "After Party," and it's where we celebrate a job well done, giving details of how things went. I send one of these communications after events such as Open Houses or Field Days, after a fundraising effort, and even at the conclusion of every school year. The emails can be brief; the purpose is to express gratitude to the people who made the event possible, to share the success of the event, and to reiterate how this event or initiative was central to your vision of school improvement—in short, you're stating why it all mattered. With the busyness of our day-to-day roles, it is easy for us to move on to the next thing as soon as one big event is completed. But pausing to send an email with highlights (how much money we raised, how many parents were in attendance, how the children felt about Field Day) streamlines the messaging throughout the building.

Implement Regular Communications

Inspired by *Motivating and Inspiring Teachers* (2009), I use a "Weekly Bulletin," which goes out each weekend. It has evolved over time: at first, it was just me writing all the different sections like a mini newspaper. I would open it with a "Letter from the

Principal" highlighting important information and reminders, motivating staff. I'd write a section about Social Emotional Learning in which I'd share information about our Positive Behavioral Interventions and Supports (PBIS) program, share external services available for students and families, and/or give suggestions for Restorative Practices in the classroom. There is also a Weekly Calendar, including upcoming events beyond the immediate week, and a Shout-Outs section to express gratitude and appreciation to staff members doing amazing things above and beyond the contractual "call of duty." It also includes pictures of our students and staff with captions celebrating the various things happening around the building.

When you share bulletins regularly, it sends the message that communication is a priority, and it also indirectly gives staff members a glimpse into what you think is important, what you think is worth celebrating. Of course, these things can only be highlighted in the bulletin if you are aware they are happening.

The bulletins can highlight the very best things in your school and celebrate the good things staff members are doing. By creating this weekly visual publication, it helps build the narrative amongst your staff that great things *are* happening in your school; you are not the outcast school you'd been made to feel like. LOOK at these amazing children participating in project-based learning experiences in Mr. Rashad's class. LOOK at the way Miss Jackson is facilitating collaborative groups in her Math classroom! Try these ideas. Be proud of the great things happening. You rock!

Three Tips for Effective Weekly Bulletins:

1. *Quantity Can Crush Quality*. Originally, I felt proud that I provided tons of info in the bulletins. When teachers asked me a question, I'd reply "it was in the bulletin!" which I'm sure was universally beloved. What I wasn't banking on was that most people are checking their email on the go, either on a Sunday night while preparing lunches for their family, via cellphone, or on a Monday morning when they return to school and are preparing lessons. It was a lot of information at once,

and I needed to be sensitive to that fact. Being selective about what made "the cut" into the Weekly Bulletin is critical, but giving teachers time to review the bulletin is also important. Teachers know that they are responsible for all the information contained within the Weekly Bulletins. We now save these bulletins in our online handbook so that teachers have a starting point to look for any references or guidelines when sitting down to complete their work.

2. *Let Others Have Input.* The principal is not the only leader in a school; there are many areas in which I'd rather hear directly from the School Nurse, or the School Psychologist, as they are the experts. If we're rolling out a new math program, I'd prefer that the Math Coach take the lead on explaining it. I had to resist the urge to be in control of every area, and instead make sure to lean on my in-house experts and leaders. A few years after cranking out those dense Weekly Bulletins each weekend, I created a roll-up document for all my in-house leaders: the Wellness Team (School Psychologist, School Social Worker, School Nurse, School Counselor), my Instructional Leadership Team (my Reading and Math Coaches, my Multilingual Learners Coach), and my Assistant Principal. Each person had a section on this document to share updates, reminders, or valuable information. Now, teachers were receiving information about our current math data directly from the Math Coach. Now, teachers were given a list of Tier 2 & Tier 3 behavioral supports directly from our School Psychologist. Later, as we formed a teacher leadership team in our school, we also created a section in the bulletin for this Laboratory Team of teachers to share ideas, successes, and challenges. They would also offer to open their classroom doors if any of their peers wanted to observe something new they were trying or wanted to collaborate on planning units or lessons. The bulletin suddenly became a community effort, not a top-down oversized memo from the boss. I was still able to manage the tone and the types of things we highlighted

and celebrated, but teachers were taking the lead on sharing timely and pertinent information with all staff.

3. *Include a Shout-Out Section.* One section that I was particularly proud of was on the last page of the bulletin: "Faculty Shout-Outs!" In this section, I'd highlight three to four people who had gone "above and beyond" in some way, thanking them for their contribution, or dedication, or hard work. Some actual examples from my first few years:

Kelly Burrows: Thank you for your dedication to students; from staying after school for a 5:00 meeting to your detailed paperwork advocating for these children. It matters.

Tina Stevenson: Thank you to Tina for organizing the holiday gala! Events like this are so important to building a strong school culture. Your hard work did not go unnoticed. We all appreciate your organizational skills and your desire to make this a FUN place to work! Many thanks.

Karl Adams: Thank you, Karl, for taking the lead on a free field trip opportunity for our students. Mr. Adams secured 80 free tickets for our fifth graders to attend a Christmas performance. Karl is always on the lookout for opportunities for our students. Karl, thank you so much for going the extra mile for OUR STUDENTS!

Shout Outs Gone Wrong: How I Learned to Adjust to Feedback

In writing the shout outs in my Weekly Bulletins, I wanted to make sure that people who went above and beyond felt appreciated. What I did not count on was how it may make others feel. One day, a fourth grade teacher named Bonnie asked me if she could speak with me in my office. A bit of context: Bonnie was a tough customer. She rarely smiled, often complained, and had interpersonal issues with many staff members. When she called the office to ask to speak with me, she had a familiar dissatisfied tone in her voice, and taking this meeting was the last thing I wanted to do on a busy Monday. Curiosity and wanting to "get it over with" won out, and I asked her to come down on her planning period in about an hour.

Bonnie strode into my office in with a huge pile of paper and sat down at my table. She asked me, "Courtney, how do you determine who gets a shout out each week?" I looked at the pile of papers and realized she had printed out every single Weekly Bulletin of the year so far. At three to four pages each, the pile was substantial. She had highlighted all the shout-outs I had written so far and had tallied up how many shout outs each staff member had gotten. She was angry, furious even, that she hadn't gotten one yet that year. She pointed out all the reasons for recent staff shout-outs: staying late to set up a family dance, coaching the basketball team voluntarily after school, planting flowers in our garden on a day off. . . . She snapped at me, "I don't live close by the school. I cannot stay late and do these things. How about someone like me? I plan my lessons. I work hard. I differentiate instruction! I do everything that is expected of me. No shout out for that!?"

Initially I was taken aback—is she serious? These are meant to be fun pats on the back. A nice way to highlight the things that are happening for our school that most staff members may not know about. A way for me to show appreciation while also informing the staff at large of all the wonderful things happening around our campus, and hopefully inspiring others to get involved, and show-casing the dedication of their colleagues.

Bonnie was very serious. She also went so far as to point out that two of the teachers whom I had given frequent shout-outs to *"don't even like you very much!"* which I thought was a particularly nice touch, as she sat in my office ripping apart what was meant to be an innocent, positive, celebratory initiative that I had created. I remember responding to Bonnie that the point of shout-outs was to be celebratory, spread positivity, not to praise teachers that like me; this fell on deaf ears. Bonnie was very adamant that she deserved a shout-out. I tried meeting her in the middle and admit-ting that she could have a point, and I apologized for "falling into a pattern of recognizing things that happened outside of school hours" and that it wasn't intentional. I said she was certainly correct that hardworking teachers all deserve to be celebrated.

I was so dejected by this meeting that long after Bonnie left my office, I could not shake the feelings of being misunderstood and also being pretty annoyed that Bonnie was complaining about something meant to be so positive.

But sometimes uncomfortable events can unintentionally lead to great ideas. As a result of my conversation with Bonnie, I decided to leave the Shout-Out section in the hands of all staff. When I brought this up to Bonnie, she seemed mollified. In fact, I started loving the idea myself; it would be wonderful to read the ways in which my staff showed love and appreciation to each other. That weekend, in the Shout-Out section of the bulletin, I wrote:

> *Starting next week, I'd like to change this Shout-Out section to be written by you. Faculty Shout-Outs will be written **about** you, **by** you! There will be a box placed in the main office and the teachers' lounge where you can write up a shout-out and drop it in . . . Each Friday I'll collect and publish them in this section. You can also email shout-outs to me. It is my hope that you all have a voice in celebrating the wonderful things that are happening at our school. What I see is only a portion of what goes on in a day. PLEASE share the successes and joys that happen in your daily experiences . . . colleagues lending a hand, going above and beyond, making a difference, etc.*
>
> *This week, I want to give a shout out to everyone who dressed up for 80s Day on Thursday. What a fun day! We rocked out during all three lunches and had a blast with the kids. 80s trivia will continue up until the 89th day of school!*

Sure enough, staff members responded. I received emails or text messages each week, with positive and celebratory shout-outs to share in the bulletin; it warmed my heart and filled me with so much pride. I especially loved reading the shout-outs that used similar language and structure to the shout-outs I used to write. Seeing staff members use phrases such as "above and beyond" and "making a difference" let me know that what I had started, stuck. It worked, and now was the perfect time to let the teachers take it and run with it. *They didn't need me to manage positivity anymore.*

I believe that Bonnie's feelings about shout outs were likely not shared by most of my faculty. No one else had ever said anything to me regarding the shout-out section, other than "thanks for the shout out!" as we passed each other in the halls. However, the new style of letting staff members shout each other out was still an improvement. No matter how we got there, I'm glad we did.

Proofreading Your Communications: The Three-Read Protocol

When writing staff memos on any topic, whether it's state testing schedules or upcoming Field Day logistics, the tone and reminders can be intended in one way but received in a completely different way. Think of reading this line from a State Testing memo as an administrator:

"When students complete the test session, they must read a book. They cannot play games online or use their computers."

Makes sense—we don't want other students to see a classmate playing on the computer as soon as they finish the test then rushing so that they do so too. The memo clearly outlines what students should not be doing. This line was written with purely proactive intent, so that if a student asked their teacher if they can go online when they're finished, all teachers knew that this was not an option.

Most teachers will read it, nod, and keep reading.

But some teachers may read that and take this away: "She means me! Last year I had a few students go on the computer. She's so passive aggressive. Just tell me directly instead of shaming me in a staff memo."

Some teachers may read it and think: "I wonder who let their students go on the computer last year? Wow—I bet it was Stacey!" and discuss this further with their colleagues.

Lastly, imagine if that email were forwarded to a community member, district administrator, etc. It could also appear that we are not or at one point were not complying with testing conditions, and that possibly teachers were not following directives in past years. "Why would she mention playing games online? Is anyone checking on this school?"

We should aim to treat everyone like our best teacher. And this is true! However, when sending out communication to all staff, I have expanded on that by creating something that my former Assistant Principal and I lovingly nicknamed, "The Three-Read Protocol." We'd write an email or a memo—as benign as we thought it might be—and read it *three times* before sending: once as our Best Teacher, once as our Most Negative Teacher (the one who could find an insult in "Happy Birthday"), and once as if the email or memo were leaked to the general public. In doing this, we were able to fine-tune the way we messaged important information to all staff in an effort to not create unnecessary emotion.

I read my emails and memos once as Christine (hard worker, takes a lot of pride in her work, each year her students show growth and achievement), then as Bonnie (takes everything personally, feels that administrators are out to get her), and then one more time as if the email were printed on the district web page just to check for tone and neutrality. You don't want to accidentally write anything that could be misconstrued or taken out of context.

I've learned that a great way to communicate expectations is to write everything in the positive tone. "When students complete their test session, they must read a book. Please make sure students have a few different books to choose from, already at their desks. This is the only option for student work once they have finished their test. Thank you so much for preparing our students to do their best on the State Test!"

Keeping It Positive

Earlier, we mentioned a TED Talk by Rita Pierson, "Every kid needs a champion." In it, she gives the example of a student who got almost every single math problem wrong on a 20-question test. But instead of writing that the child had gotten 18 problems wrong, she wrote "+2" and circled it at the top. She says, "Minus 18 sucks all the life out of you. But plus 2 says, I'm not all bad!"

That became the way I tweaked my wording to staff. Rather than writing in the Weekly Bulletin "19 Days Until Summer Vacation!" I would write, "19 Days Left to Make a Difference!" or "19 Days Left to Enjoy the Classroom Family You Have Created." Just simple twists on the wording put the students and their experience first.

Is it a bad thing for teachers to be excited for summer vacation? Absolutely not. But you don't want a desire to high-tail out of your school to become the only way people view the final weeks. For many of our students, summer is not the exciting time for family vacations or outdoor adventures that it is in other communities; it can be a time of great uncertainty. Meals may become less regular and less filling. Their relationship with their teacher or support staff in the building may be their most stable or positive relationship. I never wanted the students to sense that we were excited for a school year to be over. We were working to build something and needed to eliminate the climate where teachers would exclaim "179 to go!" on the first day of school.

When we would receive news of our data dropping, whether on a state test or district progress monitoring tool, it was natural for staff and administration to feel dejected. Keeping "+2!" in mind, I always tried to highlight the things that had gone well first so that the message was not that everything we were doing was bad. The staff had lived through years of academic decline and being the lowest performing school in the state. I was entering this building at a time where people felt that nothing was going right, and that was all they ever heard from the state or district. They weren't used to being celebrated; it had been years of constant bad news. So with Rita's advice for her math student in mind, I have always tried to frame our bad news with something good or positive.

When Communication Needs to Be in Person

Timeliness and urgency matter. Student fighting, school ratings being published in the newspaper, a new Superintendent, school closures, the addition/removal of important school programming—anything that could cause criticism, fear, anxiety, or unnecessary drama amongst your staff should be handled with immediate, clear, and often in-person communication, which eliminates the confusion. I'll use a real-life emergency drill scenario as an example, but this lesson applies in any scenario in which an event occurs that may make staff upset, uncomfortable, or anxious.

During recess, a teacher walks the office to report hearing the sound of "something like fireworks" going off a few streets away. At the same time, your cell phone rings and it's the local Sergeant on the police force, directing you to bring all students inside immediately and go into a lockdown.

This scenario is all too familiar at schools across America. When practicing emergency drills, or entrenched in a real crisis, tensions can run high amongst staff and students. During a practice drill—especially a pre-announced one—it's much easier for cool heads to prevail, as staff members are aware that there is no safety threat. When a member of the administrative team announces a lockdown that nobody had forewarning about, staff become immediately on edge. Especially if they heard the "fireworks" or are aware that there was a neighborhood incident.

Things move quickly during a lockdown scenario: having facilitated several in the past decade, I know firsthand how chaotic it can be to try to manage the process while maintaining contact with emergency personnel and district supervisors. Meanwhile, the staff members in your building who are charged with keeping little ones safe and calm—5 years old or 15 years old, they're all little ones—are not always able to be kept up to date with the status of the situation.

When the emergency drill has ended, the normal process is that a member of the Crisis Team or a police officer moves about the building, unlocking classroom or office doors personally to announce the all-clear. As I open doors and greet classes who are hiding in the closet in the dark, I always use a calm and reassuring tone and compliment them with something like "great job, Room 203! You were so quiet I didn't even know you were in here!" This usually gets the students smiling a bit again. It's hard to have in-depth conversations with teachers, however, so the exchange is pretty quick, as I move along to unlock the next room.

To maintain control of the narrative and respect your staff by keeping them as informed as possible, you can offer the opportunity to debrief after such a tense situation. On the afternoon announcements, I will say that "there will be a brief staff meeting for anyone who can stay 5–10 minutes after school to debrief on the afternoon's emergency drill." I always say that I completely understand if you cannot stay on such short notice. But they all will; they're dying to talk about it. Let's face it: many of them have *already* been texting each other or checking social media for reports from local news outlets. Some of them are so tech-savvy that they already know the whole story, or they know a member of the police force and have already gained insight as to what happened in the neighborhood a few hours earlier.

I know that time is of the essence for me to share the following:

♦ What triggered the drill
♦ What steps the school took
♦ Feedback from the drill itself, including compliments or areas for growth
♦ Next steps

And I know that time is of the essence because I learned right away that if I don't hold the meeting, they will hold the meeting for me.

If I don't hold the meeting, they will hold the meeting for me. What does that mean? It surely does not mean that anyone on the staff will convene a meeting of his or her peers to circle up and share their lockdown procedures in order to tighten up our practice. What it does mean is that in the absence of leadership, people will follow the loudest voice. If even one person is critical of the way the lockdown was handled, if even one person repeats something they heard happened without verifying the truth of the statement, these are the messages your staff will receive. Even if you wait until the next morning, this gives staff time to go home and formulate their own criticisms, fears, concerns, and complaints over something that may not even be true.

Calling all staff together for a few minutes at the end of the day gives you the opportunity to share your point of view of the event and communicate the pertinent information with your staff. Imagine the whole staff gathering at the end of the day and you say:

Thanks, everyone, for staying for a few minutes this afternoon. I won't keep you long. Thank you for a job well done during this afternoon's lockdown. At approximately 1:00 this afternoon, Sgt. Williams called to direct me to bring all the students inside from recess and go into lockdown. I went outside to alert the play yard to line up and re-enter the building while Secretary Rosie put the building in lockdown. Those of you who were outside—grades 2 and 3—thank you for your quick hustling to get the children inside. Those of you in classrooms—great job following the procedure.

The Crisis Team secured the building. During the lockdown, I stayed in contact with Sgt. Williams. He let me know that three blocks away, a passenger in one car shot at another car. They pursued the vehicle and made an arrest. They believe the incident was isolated, and not related to any school in the area. The suspect is in custody. We took the building out of lockdown at 1:15 pm. Mrs. Andrews, thank you for reminding me that you need a new key for your classroom. We'll get you a new key by tomorrow. Great idea to take your students and join Mrs. Perry in her classroom.

That's all I know right now. If you have any questions about the process we followed, or feedback for me, I'm here as long as you need me.

Every time I've done this, there are questions. Staff want to clarify the way they followed the procedure, to make sure they got it right. Teachers sometimes offer additional information they may have read online or gotten from friends at large. Sometimes, teachers have concerns or questions about the way something was handled by our team, or by the district or local law enforcement. I either answer them as best as I can or thank them for bringing the concern to me and let them know I will let them know once I am better informed. Many times, teachers have suggestions on ways that we can tighten our procedure if a similar scenario ever happens again. I always feel better about managing these discussions and being present for the first opportunity that the staff is gathering to discuss the event, so that any potential/future criticisms first show themselves as questions that I am given the opportunity to respond to.

Without this quick meeting at the end of the day, a few teachers could have gone out for coffee or chatted on their rides home. I could imagine statements such as:

> *"I heard the sound of shots. I think someone shot toward the recess yard because everyone came running inside!"*
>
> *"They didn't really wait that long before taking the building out of lockdown, how did they know everything outside was all set? I think she rushed it."*
>
> *"During the lockdown, Mrs. Andrews took her whole class into Perry's room. What was that about? Was Andrews's side of the building unsafe? Did she see something out her window?"*

This is a very extreme example that I hope many administrators never have to face. I use this scenario because it has happened to me, and if it works in serious situations such as this, imagine how helpful it is to gain control of panic and anxiety when staff hears things about common situations such as classroom cuts, program changes, tuition increases, and so on. Anything that can cause teachers to complain, anything that can chip away at culture and make people feel less "safe," emotionally or physically, deserves that 5–10 minutes.

Final Thoughts

Communication is key, whether you're providing details of an upcoming event or a quick wrap up, to show your staff that it was worth it. Keep it positive and consider the three-read protocol to consider how it can be received by different constituents. And finally, remember that some communications need to be handled instantly, in person. When things go wrong, hold the meeting before it is held for you. Always remember, "In the absence of communication, the rumor mill will fill the void."

9

Celebrating and Recognizing Your Staff

When we have a lot of fires to put out, the best teachers in the building often get ignored. What motivation will our best teachers have to stay if they feel unseen? Deep down, our best teachers know why more of our time is spent elsewhere, but the nature of our best teachers is that they are always seeking to improve. They desire feedback. They want to be acknowledged and appreciated. When you're working to turn around culture and climate, your best teachers need to lead the way.

Ten Ways to Acknowledge Greatness

1. Share Pictures and Videos of Excellent Teaching in Action

One thing I started to do in my Weekly Bulletins was to share pictures I had taken during the week with captions that praised the work being done in classrooms. For example, if I had entered a third-grade classroom during a great writing lesson, I'd snap a picture and then share it in the bulletin with the caption, "Third-grade writers love to share their stories with a partner. Excellent idea to have students pair up to give each other feedback, Miss Jackson!" This worked well for a few reasons: one, everyone loves to see pictures of our students in the bulletin—they are the reason why we do what we do. Two, it's sometimes impossible

DOI: 10.4324/9781003321323-13

for teachers to get beyond the four walls of their classroom and know what's going on in any other classroom, especially at different grade levels. These pictures served as a peek inside other teachers' learning spaces, often sharing ideas and inspiration. Three, it reinforced the great things that are happening in our building in an effort to set an expectation and hopefully replicate the great lessons or great ideas in other classrooms. I'd name the strategy or the standard being highlighted and name the teacher.

I still get text messages every Sunday as teachers open the bulletin and see pictures of their students: "Thank you for sharing the picture of Jordana and Angel during math groups!" It's such a quick, easy way to validate great things happening in your building. I also get texts all throughout the week from teachers sharing pictures of sweet moments, exciting group projects, or just adorable photo opportunities. If a teacher texts me a picture of something that happened in their classroom, I know that they're feeling proud and are looking for feedback and validation from me. I always write back eventually, and if I can put it in the Weekly Bulletin, I will. The culture of sharing and celebrating our students through pictures is contagious now!

2. Find Things to Celebrate Schoolwide

You are your school's head cheerleader. Like it or not, you're captain of the squad. This is not to say you are your school's *lone* cheerleader; that is a significant difference and could be unsustainable for the long term—not a situation you want to find yourself in. But being your school's *head* cheerleader means that you set the tone in terms of celebrating successes or wins, bringing people together when times are tough, and pumping people up when challenging days are upon you. It's a tenet of building a positive school culture and climate to celebrate every win, no matter how big or small.

When I took over as principal, I spent time during the summer months looking over the past three years of staff attendance. I looked at trends, as well as personal attendance histories. I learned that the central point of the school year—the dark days of New England winter—was traditionally our worst attendance period. The days with the least sunlight, the cold, snowy, slushy morning commutes, and the lack of excitement all contributed to a real dip in January and February. One idea I had to combat that "dreary" time of year was to celebrate with some fun, for both students and staff. If you think of a 180-day school year in a linear way, you have the first 80 days: this took us to the holidays, and into January. The first 80 days contains the excitement of September, the fun of Fall, the chaotic buzz of the holidays, and the relaxing return after New Year's. Then the next 20 days takes us from mid-January to the end of February. This time of year is often dark, cold, and a bit depressing. Then the last 80 days: the springtime beauty and excitement, longer sunlight, outdoor activities, the promise of summer right around the corner, and end-of-the-year activities.

I referred to that time period in the midst of Days 80–100 as "the dark days in February." What could we do to keep that September, excited feeling, from day 80 to day 100? We started a tradition of celebrating the 80th Day with "80s Day." It was a Spirit Day for students and staff, where all were encouraged to dress in stereotypical 80s clothing and accessories. During lunch in the cafeteria, 80s music blares through the speakers, and we encourage students to dance and enjoy the music while they eat. It's a nonstop party—the cafeteria workers often come out and dance along with us! We added to that by starting the daily announcements with a short burst of a recognizable 80s song on the loudspeaker, and an 80s trivia question for our staff members. If staff members know the answer, they submit it with their name into a raffle basket on the main office counter. During the afternoon announcements, a winner is chosen, their name is announced, and a small prize is waiting for them in the main office. We extended this fun day by continuing the morning music bursts, the daily trivia question and raffle winners, for each day of school, Day 80–Day 89. On the 90th Day of School, we do it all over again by hosting 90s Day (outfits, cafeteria dance party, daily music, and trivia) and continue this pattern until Day 99. On the 100th Day of School, teachers at various grade levels celebrate that with all sorts of well-known fun activities. And before you know it, we made it through the mid-year slump and had a lot of fun doing it.

We're not suggesting that your staff members with chronic absenteeism issues are going to stop calling out needlessly because they can't wait to hear a 10-second snippet of Van Halen right before the Pledge of Allegiance on a snowy Monday. What we are suggesting is that events and activities like this bond a faculty and strengthen the team. Everyone feels a little bit more a "part of something" when there's an energy, a vibe, and positive momentum.

3. Make People Feel Special

During our first year back from Covid, our school nurse had the unenviable task of weekly testing, daily quarantine paperwork, constantly swabbing noses, isolating students and staff, and so much more. Our school nurse needed to take some time off at the end of the school year for a minor surgery and would be out from late March until June. It didn't sit well to let the MVP of this crazy, unprecedented school year quietly leave without proper recognition. I could certainly get her some flowers, write her a nice card. I could organize the front office staff to all go in on a larger floral arrangement, and maybe have a cake. There are many wonderful, yet typical ways to show appreciation and wish someone well. However, nothing felt right except for really *celebrating* Cora, making a big deal out of honoring the overwhelming workload she carried for the past year. So we decided to bombard her at dismissal with cards, flowers, and some confetti to say goodbye on her way out the door. But the day of the surprise, Nurse Cora mentioned that she had an appointment immediately after school and would need to leave right at the bell. "Of course, Cora, no problem," I said—but oh what a problem it was. The faculty knew we'd be gathering in the foyer at dismissal; many had brought in gifts, flowers, confetti cannons . . . uh-oh. What an awkward celebration it would be without the guest of honor.

After some quick brainstorming, my Assistant Principal and I came up with a workaround: what if we fake an evacuation drill sometime in the afternoon? Get everyone outside—socially distanced, of course—and expand the celebration to not only just teachers in the foyer but the students as well! It just made sense. Sometimes, things work out even better than you could plan. I sent an email to the staff so that everyone would be informed and no one would panic.

The email read:

Change of plans. Nurse Cora has an important appointment immediately after school today. SO, we are going to pull an evacuation drill around 2:00. It's the only way. Bonus: this way the TAs who are also bus monitors won't miss out!! I won't sound the fire alarm as to not scare our students. Please bring your cards or flowers or whatever you have for Cora with you! I'll bring the balloons.

DO NOT LINE UP ON THE FIELD *[this is our normal evacuation routine, which would have spread everyone out much too far apart to celebrate]. Line up at your dismissal locations on the blacktop. Spread OUT! If you aren't sure where to stand, simply find a spot not too close to another class. Once we are outside, teachers can gather around Nurse Cora on the blacktop and we can set off the confetti cannons and wish her well.*

Please tell your neighbors, text your colleagues, as I know not everyone checks email as frequently as others. This is going to be fun. And now our students can celebrate Nurse Cora too!

And celebrate we did. When I came on the intercom to announce that we'd need to evacuate the building, I saw classrooms walking outside in a rush, but with slight smirks on all the children's faces rather than the confusion and panic that can sometimes set in during emergency drills. I saw Nurse Cora grab her black leather emergency bag and dash out to the blacktop. Once we were outside, I blew the whistle and announced the real reason we were outside. Teachers gathered around Cora and shot off confetti cannons, presented her with flowers, cards, beverages. The kids clapped and cheered amidst the balloons and streamers—what a moment. Nurse Cora was visibly touched, and it felt good to unite our school around showing appreciation and honoring the hard work Cora has always done for us. Our school is nestled into a neighborhood; we are a part of the block, not set off the street as some schools are. We were in full view of parents and neighbors who could see what we were doing; some came outside to join us and wish Nurse Cora well, too. Moments like this reminded me not only of what we were building together, but what we had already built as well. We had become a family. Would teachers and students have presented Nurse Cora with cards or gifts since she was leaving, without this ceremony? Probably! Bringing everyone together, however, created a moment in time that Cora, her colleagues, and the students won't soon forget.

Why I think this story is important to tell: Leaders can say that their school is a team and say that their school is a family. Those are words; it's the actions that people remember. Making a valued member of our team feel irreplaceable and special— that's walking the walk. People want to feel seen, valued, and appreciated. This can be hard to do well in the hustle and bustle of our busy workdays, but it's important to grasp the opportunity when you can! Don't ever get so busy that you don't see these opportunities in front of you.

"People who feel appreciated will always do more than is expected." I've read this quote hundreds of times, but not until I became a school administrator did the quote fully resonate. It goes hand in hand with what Maya Angelou said: "I've learned that people will forget what you said, people will forget what you did, but people will never forget how you made them feel." We shouldn't just do nice things so that people will work harder; we should do them because educators deserve to be appreciated and to feel valued. If people work harder and strive to be even better than the day before, that benefits the school and most of all, our students. A simple compliment goes a long way.

4. Awesome Citations
Once, while I was browsing through a gift shop, I saw a cute "While You Were Out" memo pad that a secretary may use to deliver phone messages. It reads "Awesome Citation" across the

top and has a checklist of all sorts of fun, positive traits that you can check off and write a personal note. I started using this pad to leave brief, positive "Awesome Citations" in staff mailboxes when they aren't expecting it. Here's the kicker: I left these notes in staff members' mailboxes who would not necessarily expect a compliment or praise, teachers whom I may have had to call in the past for unacceptable behavior or excessive absences. Rather than let those incidents get between us, I tried to include those teachers in the positivity as well. Whenever there is something positive to recognize, go for it. Look for the good parts, even if you have to squint.

5. The Goal Bell

My passion for celebration reverberated throughout the staff, starting with my Assistant Principal. She was young, new, and eager to learn everything about how to turn around a school. She also brought some ideas and initiatives with her from the school where she had just completed her latest teaching assignment, the best of which was The Goal Bell.

The idea was simple: we hung a bell in the main foyer, and every time a student achieved a goal—personal, academic, behavioral—that student had the opportunity to ring the bell. Teachers and students quickly embraced the new initiative and began celebrating in the main foyer a few times a week. One student rang the bell in front of his whole class because he had gotten a high score on a state assessment. Some students began to ring the bell when they'd move from level to level in our reading program. Every few days, we'd hear the Goal Bell ringing out in the main foyer and we tried to capture these moments in pictures whenever we could.

As with any shiny, new initiative, use of the Goal Bell started out strong—it sounded like wedding bells clanging around the clock at first—dipped a little bit over the year, and then would come back in spurts as teachers remembered to celebrate daily milestones and goal setting with their students. We'd remind staff in the Weekly Bulletin to motivate students with the Goal Bell, and they would. It was a cute, positive initiative, and I am so grateful to Samantha for bringing this idea to our school, as it really fit perfectly to our "family" vibe that we'd worked so hard to cultivate for the past several years.

Years later, on the last day of work for one of our TAs, he asked if we could announce to the whole faculty to meet up briefly in the foyer at dismissal time so he could say goodbye. Victor had a larger-than-life personality and a smile to match. He was everyone's friend and was a wonderful presence in the building. We would all miss him very much, and of course I agreed to announce that everyone should congregate in the foyer at the end of the day to say goodbye.

The end-of-day bell rang, and the faculty started to make their way back inside to the foyer. I expected Victor to make some jokes, maybe make a small speech, and leave with a smile. Vic approached the Goal Bell, and to the everyone's surprise, started to tell us all that he would be ringing the Goal Bell today because he had something personal to share: he had beaten cancer. He announced, "The reason I want to ring this bell today is that I've just learned that I'm cancer free."

For an instant, the foyer was completely silent. Many staff members had no idea this was something Vic had been dealing with. Within seconds, the foyer erupted in claps, cheers, and whistles. Vic continued that he loved being a Teacher Assistant with our team because he never felt like it was teachers on one side and TAs on the other. He said he always truly felt like he was part of a family at this school. He then leaned toward the bell and gave it a very hearty shake, and the bell resounded through the hallways. He called "I love you all!" as he walked out the door that last time.

It was powerful. Celebrating beating cancer with the Goal Bell. This moment moved several of us to tears. We had something special here. Vic wanted to share this great news, and he wanted to ring that bell!

6. Teacher Appreciation Week

Every year, I make a big deal out of Teacher Appreciation Week. Teachers should feel valued and cared for every day, so during that week I try to ham it up a bit with fun daily puns and a small token or gift. Teachers groan, but they smile too—I think they like it, but they also probably call me corny behind my back—I don't mind! What's nice is that it's consistent; they know that every year, we've embarked upon Pun Week! It's just a minute or two out of their day as the administrative team stops into classrooms and recites a silly pun to teachers and support staff. Think "you're the balm!" alongside a small tube of ChapStick.

One year I thought of using our text messaging app to send a message to parents that it was Teacher Appreciation Week and asking them to reply back with a "Shout Out" or a note of appreciation for any teachers at our school. I logged back onto the app about an hour after sending the Teacher Appreciation message. I had at least 40 new texts! Each parent received this message individually—there were over 40 parents who wanted to shout out a teacher just because they thought they were worth it.

Texts were coming in fast and furious, full of love and appreciation for our teachers. When I logged back in later that evening, I had over 150. Each text I copied and pasted into a document and listed the parent who submitted it, often including emojis and even pictures. Remember: more than half of the parents at my school have a first language other than English, but our app translates all texts to the parents' preferred language. It was very touching to read messages in English that were sent in Spanish, Pashto, Quiché, and Arabic, to know that the power of great teacher appreciation can transcend linguistic boundaries.

As I was compiling the running list of parent shout outs, I started to see a pattern: parents were sending these lovely messages for the classroom teachers, and the specialist team—Music, PE, Art, Library—was unintentionally being forgotten. A few days later, I sent another text soliciting a shout out for our amazing specialist team. Sure enough, parents responded with thoughtful and touching messages about those hardworking staff members, too.

On the Friday of that week, I sent the document out to the entire staff as a Google Doc. I presented it as a "gift" from the parents to our teachers. Since it was a shared document, I could see teachers popping up one at a time, viewing the document. During the afternoon and at dismissal, I had several teachers tell me that they cried joyful tears reading the shout-outs.

It was the best gift I ever gave my teachers and it 1) had nothing to do with me whatsoever, and 2) cost no money. My text to parents and follow-up texts only facilitated a channel of appreciation between parents and teachers. The parents are the ones who stepped up to the plate.

Another hallmark of our Teacher Appreciation Week is a tradition called "Cheers for Our Peers," where we put a clear jar out on the office counter with ribbons and a colorful sign that says "Leave a CHEER for your PEER!" I cut up dozens and dozens of colorful strips of paper and leave them in a basket by the jar. Any staff member can write a compliment, thoughtful note of gratitude, or a shout-out to any person on the staff. The jar fills up each day, and during the afternoon announcements I'll pull one "cheer" randomly from the jar and read it on the PA system, such as "this cheer comes to us from Paola Santiago. She says: Thank you to Amanda Barker for always being available to collaborate and plan with me before school. I have gotten so many great ideas from you this year!" Then both Paola and Amanda win a daily raffle prize. It could be as simple as a candy bar or a coffee gift card, or something a bit more out-of-the-box such as a ticket to park in a special parking spot for a week or 30 minutes of coverage by the Assistant Principal.

At the end of the five-day week, ten people have won a daily raffle: the writer of each day's Cheer and the receiver of each Cheer. I then take all the Cheers that were written and file them in the mailbox of the recipient. What a nice surprise for teachers to check their mail and find such nice things their colleagues wrote about them. Again, my input was minimal. I just acted as facilitator.

7. Use Social Media

One way to show, not tell, your staff how much you appreciate them is by highlighting them outside of your organization, such as by using social media. Every time I share something positive that is happening in a teacher's classroom or something exciting that staff members are working on, I share it, tag the district, and use our school's hashtag. It's part of our branding efforts, but it's also true because I am proud of the things my teachers are doing. I am grateful and proud to work with so many individuals who are as committed to turning this school around as I am.

8. Seize Award Opportunities and Larger Moments

Another way I promote my teachers is by seizing larger opportunities to share and celebrate the good work they do. For example, our Physical Education team was working really hard "behind the scenes" to support our recess initiative PlayWorks, a program which promotes positive play, conflict-resolution skills, and team building activities. The PE team was teaching the PlayWorks games during PE class, ensuring that the recess equipment was ordered and replenished when necessary, and even facilitating staff training during our professional development days. When the PlayWorks corporation reached out to see how our school was doing with the initiative, they were impressed with the work our school had put into the program. The representative told me that they presented annual "Recess Champion" awards across the state to people who were achieving success with the program and that I should nominate my PE team. So I did! They were awarded the Recess Champion recognition, and then our school department followed suit by honoring them at a School Committee meeting. The local news came to do a short, positive story about them too, which included interviewing and highlighting our students. Our PE teachers deserved the recognition, and it also highlighted our school in a positive light. An easy but meaningful win-win.

Another example was when I nominated a teacher for a leadership award. Principals can get hundreds of emails in a day, and that's if things are going smoothly. When trying to catch up on my inbox, anything that looks like a mass/junk email is usually deleted or at the most, scanned very quickly. One day as I was checking emails, I saw a mass email from the State Department of Education asking for principals to submit the names of any teachers within the first ten years of their career who had "leadership potential." This was exactly the type of email that is easy to dismiss: it wasn't addressed to me, it went out to hundreds of principals across the state, no one would care if I deleted it and never responded. No one would notice. I had more important emails to respond to. I had deadlines!

For whatever reason that day, I decided to take the time. I submitted a name, Christine. Christine was the first teacher I hired on my first week on the job. Christine is engaging, motivated, and effective. She loves her students, loves her job, and loves being a teacher. I was happy to share her name with the state department of education as someone whom I believed had leadership qualities. I had to fill out a form with examples of how this teacher displayed leadership qualities and what made this teacher a leader in my building. Who knew what would come of that, but I felt good that I had done it. It was a small thing for me at the time, and I had forgotten all about it by the time the day ended.

A few months later, Christine approached me in the hall and showed me that she had received a large manila envelope from the State Department of Education. In the envelope was a beautiful certificate with her name on it, recognizing her as an Educational Talent Leader in our state. Christine was so proud, so honored, so touched. She showed everyone that certificate, and she deserved to feel the recognition, the pride in feeling "seen." All this from an email I could have so very easily deleted. This moment was when I learned that it's worth taking the extra few minutes to do the nice thing. It was worth it for our building's culture; great teachers like Christine feeling supported and respected by not only their principal but the state writ large.

A few months later, over the summer, I received an email from the State Department of Education asking me to fill out a few more forms about Christine. They wanted to know a bit more about student data coming out of her classroom over the past few years. I thought to myself, "Wow they're really digging deep before they give out next year's certificates!" I responded with more specific and thoughtful answers, shared some graphs with data from the past few years of reading growth . . . the emails continued, asking for more information and more student data. It all started to feel suspiciously inquisitive. And then I received the phone call that changed Christine's life: she had won the Milken Educator Award. A representative from the State Department of Education called me to inform me, and the two of us screamed on the phone like teenagers. This was unbelievable: the Milken Award?! At our little school? The school that no one wanted? On the national stage?

The Milken Educator Award is known as the "Oscar of teaching," and surprising Christine with this honor was one of the highlights of *my entire career*. To see someone so deserving, so humble, and so hardworking recognized for her pure love of teaching—and at our school! This was a turning point and a day that made every single educator at our school stand up a little taller: we were doing it. Our school was being recognized for excellence. Christine was representing not only herself—she was representing all of us. Our entire school beamed with pride that day and wrapped its arms around Christine on a day that changed her life forever.

And I could have deleted that email. *Take the time. Do the nice thing!*

9. Dance out the Door

I'm someone who appreciates order, organization, and structure. I've spent a lot of time designing safe and orderly procedures for morning arrival and afternoon dismissal. But there are two days during the school year when during dismissal all bets are off, and anything goes: the day before the winter break and the last day of school.

On these days, we have a tradition of "dancing out the door." On the day we break for the holidays in December, we play "All I Want for Christmas Is You" by Mariah Carey over the intercom system. On the last day of school, we play "Celebration" by Kool and the Gang. The songs are audible from every corner of our building, even outside on the play yard with the parents. We set the audio up so that the song plays on repeat, until the buses pull away.

Students and teachers all dance their way down the halls, down the stairs, and out the door. The members of the Wellness Team and our Leadership Team are stationed in the Main Foyer, ready to sing and dance with our students on their way out.

There's nothing else like seeing our students and teachers enjoying the moment so much. I have numerous videos that I'll treasure forever of our students and staff clapping, dancing, twirling, and laughing. In the Bus Room, we dance with students as they enter the room and proceed to their bus lines.

Something interesting has also started to happen on the last day before break and the last day of school: a significant amount of children are sometimes teary-eyed or emotional. The fact that these children feel so connected to their teachers and their school that they're sad to leave us makes me very emotional, too. We have worked so hard to create this environment for our students and to see it change from what it was in the past to what it is now gives us all a feeling of pride and accomplishment.

We work in a very transient city, with students and families moving often, either within our city, to new states, or to and from their country of origin. On this last day of school, there's always a lingering feeling inside of me that *this may be the last time we ever see Jaiden*, or *I wonder if Sarah's family are really moving back to New York*. It's a positive and upbeat tradition that the staff really enjoys, but there's also an emotional aspect to it too, as we watch our children singing dancing, twirling out the door and heading off into their futures. For all of the bittersweetness, though, it's invaluable to know that everyone who leaves our school leaves on a positive note.

10. Celebrate the End of Year!

The End of the Year Faculty Meeting is one of our school's most important traditions for unifying culture and maximizing positivity. We usually schedule this annual event one or two days prior to the actual last day of school. I start by thanking everyone for all that occurred during the year and celebrate the highlights—staff awards, school recognitions, and so on.

We got into the tradition of giving out very silly, very specific, and personal awards to staff members who can sometimes "fly under the radar." Just making sure to acknowledge people—not only our superstars or retirees but those hardworking staff members who may sometimes feel invisible. Also common was a silly award to signify something funny that had happened that not everyone is aware of. It's a vehicle for sharing a comical story to the staff as we reflect on the year. We're really giving the award just to share a fun, feel-good story from the year that most people may not know about.

One of our tongue-in-cheek accolades, the Usain Bolt Award, we gave to our School Psychologist, Mr. Donaldson. Mr. Donaldson was a very quiet man: bright, well liked, and studious. Very unassuming and always very calm. We announced that Mr. Donaldson would be getting the Usain Bolt award, and when Mr. D came up to accept his certificate, he was already laughing because he knew why he was getting this. My Assistant Principal and I told the story of how one day, a kindergartener took off running out of the cafeteria, and we were worried he would run right out the door—something he had already tried early that day. Mr. Donaldson sprinted after him and successfully stopped him from exiting the building. My AP and I, while relieved that the student was safe, could not focus on anything other than what we had just witnessed. We laughed for what felt like the rest of the day about how Mr. D ran out of the cafeteria so fast that he was like a blur. The faculty enjoyed the story and roared with laughter. Mr. Donaldson graciously accepted the award and said something along the lines of, "Okay, okay, I'll start a track team next year." This way, a fun anecdote that had drawn the AP and I together with Mr. Donaldson could now be shared with the entire faculty, further bolstering our culture of community.

I then take time to sincerely acknowledge staff members who are moving on. These can be retirements, staff who are moving away, or staff who took a job elsewhere. If a member of our school family is leaving, we'll acknowledge it and wish them well. We make each person's departure a "moment" and sometimes, the staff can end up in tears when it's an especially longtime member of the family who will be leaving us. Just because someone is leaving doesn't mean that the positive impact they had on all of us leaves too.

The end of the year Faculty Meeting is so much different than Orientation Day in that people are ready to take some time off—time well-earned. Keeping that in mind, I also really want them to walk out the door to begin their summer vacation with positive thoughts of our school year, and a feeling of satisfaction on a job well done. The goal is that my staff leaves feeling appreciated, and that the school year is "wrapped up" with a feeling of pride.

To help ensure this, I always create an end of the year slideshow to celebrate all that happened during the school year. It's sweet to see pictures of teachers and students dressed up for Halloween or lined up on the first day of school. Comments usually ring out over the music such as, "Oh my gosh, remember when Roberto was on crutches? That feels like two years ago!" I make sure that every staff member and every class has representation. The next day during lunches, we'll show the students the slideshow, too. They always scream and laugh when they see themselves or their teachers on the screen. Being seen in something like that cements a student or teacher's place in our school family.

My hope is that each year, my staff create memories that will make them proud of what they accomplished. Of course, end of year staff meetings can be very sentimental too, as it always includes saying goodbye to at least one person. The trick is to keep the meeting sentimental but upbeat, and always leave 'em wanting more. Sure, no one leaves in June wanting more school, but they can leave feeling part of something special, feeling appreciated, and feeling "the vibe!"

When Celebrating Can Go Wrong

It wasn't all roses all the time — I learned some valuable lessons over the years about what *not* to do as well. What you do for any occasion should be sustainable. Don't make the mistake of a new principal trying to "wow" their new staff and go all out with a formal luncheon and manicures/massages for all staff if you cannot keep up that pace every year. Don't do something for one person that you aren't doing for everyone. I remember when one year, a young teacher lost her father. It was a shock, and everyone seemed to be talking about it—*poor Vivian. How awful.*

Many people had approached me that day, asking if I knew where the wake was being held. During the afternoon announcements, I added something like, "For anyone who will be attending the services this afternoon for Mr. Brown, it's at Such-and-Such in East Providence." I thought that might be helpful. Weeks later, I learned that another staff member in the building scoffed at my message and said, "She didn't announce that when *my* father died!" Ouch. She was right; I hadn't announced anything. This particular staff member was a bit older and was not as vocal about the passing of her father, and the staff hadn't discussed it to the extent they had been sympathizing over Vivian's loss. It certainly wasn't personal, but I have never announced something like that again, as I can imagine it probably did make others who had experienced a loss feel excluded. You learn the hard lessons by making mistakes.

Final Thoughts

There are so many ways you can celebrate and recognize your staff. We discussed ten strategies—share pictures of excellent teaching in action, find things to celebrate schoolwide, make people feel special, awesome citations, the Goal Bell, Teacher Appreciation Week, use social media, seize award opportunities, dance out the door, and celebrate the end of year. Find the strategies that work for you, considering what can be sustained and how you're including everyone.

10

Building Parent and Family Support

If family engagement is something your school is working to improve, it's probably not due to lack of effort! Depending on the community in which you work, there are several factors which may contribute to low parent engagement: parent work schedules, cultural or linguistic barriers, distance, and more. Even switching to holding meetings via Zoom or Google Meet, while helpful for busy parents, doesn't always "fix" the issue. Some families live in homes without Wi-Fi, creating another exclusionary factor. There is no perfect solution or "one size fits all" when working to create a connection among all stakeholders.

Start with Increased Access

How can you help families access you without piling more on their plates? Early on, we started a tradition of hosting a weekly "coffee hour" outside where the buses and parent cars dropped students off. We named it "Coffee by the Curb" and the original idea was just to increase access: access to a child's teachers, the principal, Specialist teachers such as Music and PE. It was simple—we'd brew coffee in a large carafe and set up outside for the 30 minutes before the bell. At first, parents were hesitant. "No thanks, I didn't bring any money!" Then they realized that it was

DOI: 10.4324/9781003321323-14

just a casual opportunity to stay connected. We're here serving coffee, available to talk about anything at all.

The event caught on. We started serving coffee to the crossing guard, bus drivers, van drivers, all parents approaching on foot—it was contagious. Some parents accepted the coffee and kept moving, others lingered and socialized with us for a few moments. It hit me a few months into this new initiative: we should be handing out school information while we're out here. We started printing out colorful slips of paper called "What's Up Wednesday" that listed four to five important upcoming events. We had it translated into Spanish as well, and each week we'd update the slip to include current important dates.

We also list where families can find us on social media at the bottom. We've provided an actual example of what we'd prepare for Coffee by the Curb. We'd print the What's Up Wednesday slip on bright, colorful paper. We did this for two reasons: one, it's appealing. Two, it served as a visual marker for those of us who were outside serving coffee. As we'd approach cars that were lined up in traffic, we'd know if someone already approached that car by spotting the brightly colored paper either in the driver's hands or on the dashboard. When it was very busy, as it often was during the last 10–15 minutes of the event as more and more students arrived to school, those colorful papers ensured that we didn't approach the same person multiple times and instead continued to approach new cars or families on foot.

We started to get to know our parents' coffee orders, too. One father used to say, "I only drink tea!" with a smile as we offered him a coffee each week. We started bringing out a thermos of hot water and a tea bag, and when we saw him coming, we'd have a hot tea ready. It was a small gesture, but he absolutely loved it. These small gestures add up and make a difference.

Engage Them in Sustained Involvement

Getting families in the door for a fun, all-school evening event such as a Harvest Festival or Valentine's Dance might not be hard. What is often tougher is engaging a core group of stakeholders to

THANK YOU FOR GETTING YOUR CHILD TO SCHOOL ON TIME!

Each Wednesday, we will be outside serving coffee and meeting with families from 8:40-9:10.
See you on Wednesdays at "Coffee by the Curb!"

School Name
"What's Up" Wednesday:

May 15th- 18th
Math RICAS Testing grades 3-5

Monday, May 29th
No School- Memorial Day

Tuesday, May 30th
Evening of the Arts 5:30-7:00

Wednesday, June 7th
Fun Family Fitness Night 5:00-6:30

Check us out on social media:

www.facebook.com/SchoolName

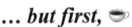 @SchoolName

... but first, ☕

¡GRACIAS POR TRAER A SU HIJO/A A LA ESCUELA A TIEMPO!

Cada miércoles, estaremos afuera sirviendo café y reuniedonos con las familias de 8:40 a 9:10.
Nos vemos los miércoles en el "Coffee by the Curb!"

Nombre de Escuela
"Que Pasa" Miercoles:

15 al 18 de mayo
Math RICAS Testing gr. 3-5

lunes, 29 de mayo
No hay escuela - Día de los Caídos

martes, 30 de mayo
La noche de las Artes

Miércoles, 7 de junio
Divertida noche familiar de ejercicios

Visítenos en las redes sociales:

www.facebook.com/SchoolName

 @SchoolName

... pero primero, ☕

Figure 10.1 Example of "What's Up Wednesday" slip

be part of any sort of Parent Teacher Committee or Organization. It's an uphill battle for any school.

We stumbled upon a great idea during one of our recruitment drives. We were holding a brand-new event: Fun Family Fitness Night, where we demonstrated some simple exercises, served healthy snacks, showcased our PlayWorks recess games, and had rooms dedicated to different physical activities. We instructed families to come dressed to work out! One room was for yoga, another for gymnastics, and in our gym, we held a Zumba class.

The Zumba instructor had a wonderful personality and a playlist of many upbeat songs, mostly in Spanish. The majority of families at my school are from Hispanophone backgrounds, yet I had never connected the dots before this night that the Zumba would be a huge hit.

Fitness Night was off to a great start, many families milling around . . . then the Zumba instructor announced class would be starting in the gym. Several staff members and students planned to participate, and we hoped that parents would join in. As we filed into the gym, water bottles in hand, towels ready, I noticed that a rush of parents were packing in, too. Not only were they entering the gym, they were wearing bright-colored Zumba outfits, spandex leggings and headbands, wrist bands—they had seen the flyer that we'd be having a Zumba class and they were excited.

We had a blast. It isn't often that I find myself dancing cha-cha or hip-hop with students, parents, and my colleagues. We danced, we exercised, we burned calories, and we had so many parents eager to participate. When it was over, I got an idea: why didn't we attach a Parent Teacher Committee meeting to the end of a Zumba class?

Fun Family Fitness Night was in June, so the following year we started fresh: monthly Parent Teacher Committee meetings with a Zumba class first, and afterwards we'd stay for healthy snacks and a brief meeting. Each month, we invited that same Zumba instructor back and parents came in droves. These moms were serious about their Zumba, and our teachers and staff were into it, too. If parents or staff didn't want to Zumba, they didn't have to; they could just come to the meeting afterward.

We found something that excited parents, something that got people in the door, and there was absolutely no need to worry about childcare, as the class was child-friendly and participation was encouraged. Parlaying this into a core group of stakeholders who were committed to meeting to discuss school improvement was easier than I could have ever hoped for.

What gets your families in the door? Depending on your community, location, school level, and demographics, the answers will vary wildly. Whatever gets people in the door, bonding your community, is a success. Getting people in the door is the first step, getting them involved comes next.

School Involvement at Home

We would like parent involvement at school. We need parent involvement at home. Though the word parent should be expanded on to include all relatives and care givers, the real difference maker is having family members involved at home with their children and their learning from Pre-K to 12th grade. At the early grades it can be as basic as sending books home with students to keep in primary grades and sharing the importance and best ways to ready the children. One school in a smaller community sent a welcome/congratulations basket when a child was born in the local hospital that included several books and a onesie with the school logo and mascot on it, and when pictures were taken of the child in it, they would share on the school website, etc. Then each year on their birthday, a card was sent to the home of the child letting them know how excited they were to have them attend in the future with a couple of other books for home reading and a stuffed mascot toy when they turned one.

At all levels, teachers can have a class social media account that shares activities, etc. that took place in class that day. Then, family members rather than asking, "What happened at school today?" can look at the feed and ask about the sweet potato experiment, mock trial, or assembly. Specific questions are much more difficult to avoid at any age!

Final Thoughts

Family involvement is tricky at many schools, and it isn't for lack of trying. Consider families' situations and how you can increase their access to the school, in ways that work for them. How can you get them in the door? And how can you connect them to the learning at home, too?

IV

Leadership Grows Leadership

11

Making Time for What Only You Can Do

When new administrators accept their first leadership job, they are normally very excited and proud. We see many people announce their new positions publicly, either on Twitter or with an email to their current staff. It's heartwarming to read these positive celebrations, and it's also a great opportunity to read the snippets of advice or lessons learned that people send them as they embark on their journeys. It can be invaluable to hear people's tried-and-true approaches to being successful in these jobs.

One of the most common truisms we see among the well-wishes goes something like, "If you're in your office, you're in the wrong place!" I couldn't agree more—how can you effect change if you're not present? I made it a point to be *in* the lunch-room, every day, every lunch. Behavioral issues in the past meant that my presence in the lunchroom would be beneficial regardless, but I also believe in the power of connecting with the students during lunches simply by being seen. I was in classrooms. I was loading buses. I was positioned in hallways during transition times. Anything I asked a teacher to do, I'd be doing it too. My hands were on everything, and I loved it. I felt like this was the only way to truly "own" what was happening at our school and make the changes necessary to improve and grow in each area.

DOI: 10.4324/9781003321323-16

Then, after the last bus pulled away, I'd log onto my computer and see that the budget was due in four days, I had about 30 new emails in my inbox, a few district offices were looking for various reports or surveys, I had three evaluations to score . . . this list, unfortunately, goes on. I was settling in to do hours of work *after work*, on my own time. And this was on the days that there were no after-school activities to attend!

I often thought of one of my best friends who works at an investment firm and specializes in financial planning. I would think: *What does a typical workday look like for Jessica?* I figured she spent a good amount of time meeting with her team, working on projects, and sending/responding to emails. She had report deadlines, too. She's a hard worker and manages a team of people like I do. All of the things that constitute a full workday for her, however— reports, meetings, emails, planning—were taking place *during* her workday. These things were taking place *after* mine. So in essence, I realized I was doing what some people's full-time jobs entailed—emails, reports, phone calls, documentation—on my own time! How could I be present during the day without giving myself an entire evening's or weekend's worth of tasks?

Prioritize Your Presence

It's not an easy balance, and it's not something that will ever feel the same from one school to the next. A number of different factors determine how visible you need to be at any given time:

◆ Staffing: Do you have an administrative team, or are you the lone administrator? If you have a team, you can spread some of the responsibility of being present amongst the group. However, delegating only works if you've taken sufficient care and time to ensure that you and your team are on the same page. What does "being present" mean to you, and how will your Assistant Principal, or Dean of Students, support you by holding the same priorities and behaviors?

◆ Safety: If something is a safety issue, don't delegate it. Whether it has to do with emergency drill planning, student safety, or other safety issues, you want to be as current with the processes in place as you can be.

◆ Urgency: Is anybody's mental or physical well-being in question? Is the Superintendent's Office following up?

◆ Deadlines: Some deadlines are federal and state mandates. These tasks should move up to the top of your priority list and may qualify as an appropriate moment to "close your door" and get some work done.

The obvious answer is for us to learn to delegate and create the kind of operations and programs in a school that can last even without our being there. Delegation—the answer to everything! The stronger and more cohesive your team is, the more you can delegate and trust them to take care of things.

The areas that most need "turning around" in your school are the areas where you should prioritize your presence. I really do believe in leading from the front and being present for your staff and students. Remember: Someone's watching, and someone cares.

Use the Gradual Release Method for Rollouts

I mentioned how dangerous and unstructured daily operations at my school were before we began the turnaround process. I'm proud of the procedures we have in place now, and I know that if I were to step away, the safe and orderly way that dismissal runs at my school would continue. This, however, was very much not the case during my first year! Had I put out the new procedure, been present for the first week or two then disappeared, the whole thing would've gone belly-up.

The gradual release method, something elementary teachers often refer to as "I do, we do, you do," became a model for my implementation practice. First, a teacher models a skill by showing the students how to do something, then doing that skill together, then releasing the child to complete the task or skill independently. I've found that in many aspects of leading operations, that's the way to go.

Being present and visible is key. It's a priority! But if the only way a system or structure will be successful is if you are in the room, that's a problem.

In my first year as principal, I was unintentionally the Lone Ranger, a solo administrator with very little leadership support during those first years of turnaround. During lunchtime, I was greeting students at the cafeteria door for every lunch period; I was on the microphone reviewing volume expectations, flow of traffic directions, and dismissal procedures. I was walking outside with each lunch period and lining them up on the recess yard. I was blowing the whistle and facilitating the lineup/transition to recess procedure. Meanwhile, the next lunch was starting inside, so I'd run back because if I wasn't there to greet the classes, they may not enter the cafeteria following the expectations we'd set. It was physically impossible to be everywhere all at once. If I received a walkie call during lunch, I'd be afraid to leave lest things descend into chaos.

Delegating some of these tasks was imperative. I'd sit down at my desk after that last bus pulled away and be faced with close to one hundred emails that I hadn't even seen. Many days, there was also a line of teachers and staff who were lingering in the main foyer or the office who wanted to touch base about something, or chat about an incident that had occurred during the day. I loved being available for them, but it'd push my "work time" back even later. Scheduling some time during the day to connect with priorities and responsibilities isn't neglectful; it's necessary.

At each lunch period, I identified one or two people who would be the leader if I wasn't at school. I made the time to explicitly review the procedure with these leaders. Once the lunch leaders felt confident in how the lunch periods are run, I'd hand the reigns over to them but stay in the cafeteria. This allowed me to "preview" what a lunch would be like on days I wasn't there and make notes of anything I should still review with them. Eventually we'd "tag team" the lunch/recess procedure: one of us would remain inside, facilitating a safe and orderly lunch dismissal, while the other was outside, supporting a safe and orderly lineup and transition to recess. It wasn't easy for me at first, but, the goal of leaders is to create more leaders. I do, we do, you do.

Today, I have the good fortune of having an Assistant Principal and a staff who've worked with me for almost a decade and can run so many aspects of our daily operations on their own. I can hand that microphone over to almost every single supervisor and be confident that the lunchroom will be run as consistently as ever. But that's because I never went away; I continue the "I do"! Consistent modeling, being a presence—you can never hand that off for good. It takes time to release operational tasks with confidence, but this time spent on the front end pays off in dividends on the back end!

Delegate the Importance of the Task Based on the Importance of the People

It is much easier to delegate if you align the importance of the task to the importance of the people. Our mistake isn't usually delegating important tasks to ineffective people; it is usually delegating unimportant task to our most important people. This is called punishing people for being good.

Rather than asking the most talented and hard working office worker to fold and staple, ask the less talented one to fold and staple. If we ask our best people to do lower level work, it takes away from their ability to do more essential work that only they can do. And, by asking less talented people to do lower level tasks, it increases the likelihood of success and gives you the chance to reinforce their efforts. And remember, like I mentioned earlier, make sure they understand the significance of the task and how it adds to the big picture goals and successes of the school. Remember, baby steps are better than crawling.

Make Time to Take Care of Your People

Perhaps the biggest aspect of school life that principals control is taking care of their people. There's always a lot to do. New certification regulations! New laws requiring additional credits! A new program, a new Superintendent, a bus strike . . . it goes on and on. But when opportunities arise to take something off a teacher's plate or to show our teachers that we are there to support them, we should take them, no matter how busy we are.

I remember that during the winter of my first year as principal, we had an unusually high amount of snow. I started thinking of our new fire drill procedure and the fact that with about four solid feet of snow on the baseball field, we'd have to be proactive and think of an alternative fire drill gathering place. I called the staff together for a "quick, brief faculty meeting" at the end of the day. I announced on the intercom that it would only take five minutes, and that it was completely optional. I gathered everyone together in the bus room and said that I wanted to let them know that, due to the amount of snow on the ground, we'd need to create a backup plan for fire drills. I pointed out the amount of frozen snow on the field and let them know that I've been thinking of alternate routes and wanted to let them know. On any day or at any time, a student could pull the fire alarm or a real fire could break out, and we should be prepared. A few teachers said, "Oh, wow, I didn't even think of that" and we started to quickly brainstorm some ideas of places we could evacuate.

I sent a follow-up email that night with plans for us to use a recreation center nearby as our "evacuation" space. I had worked it out with their director that during inclement weather—snow on the ground, hard rain, sleet, or other reason that the field would not be appropriate to evacuate to—we'd go to their gym and line up there until it was safe to return to school.

One of my more negative teachers came up to me the next morning. I wondered what she would say to me; she usually came with problems, not solutions. She said that she had received the email with the evacuation memo attached last night. I braced myself for the kicker: what did I forget? What did I not mention that she is about to point out? She then said, "Thank you for thinking of things like that" in reference to the need to relocate our fire drill evacuation place. That was it, that was all. And she went on her way.

Try the One Day Strategy

If I'm being honest, I have not yet mastered the art of delegation and time management, and I'm not sure anyone ever does.

I'm still striving to find that mythical balance. I find that the quality of my work and the feeling of "being on top of things" directly correlates with how many extra hours I put in. It's a vicious cycle! And, truthfully, that's not a great example to set for new or early-career principals. I know how important self-care and a work/life balance is. So my advice is to pick one day. This is much like a diet, where people are trying hard to eat healthier foods and exercise more, and you often hear of them taking a "cheat day." I've been trying that with my work hours. I'll make an effort to get home at a decent hour and only whip out my laptop at night when absolutely necessary . . . but I allow myself one "cheat day" a week. Maybe it'll be Wednesday night, if my husband has a work event and I know he's not missing me for dinner. Maybe it'll be Saturday morning, when I know we have a rainy weekend ahead. If I plan to set aside time to bang out a few hours of uninterrupted work, I can more easily "shut down" at a reasonable time every other day. This strategy, combined with taking some uninterrupted time during the school day, has contributed to feeling less like I'm starting my "second full-time job" after the clock strikes 4:00 pm.

In his book *The First Days of School*, Harry K. Wong refers to the benefit of the amount of work that goes into classroom management in the first weeks of school. He says that it may *seem* like time wasted in the beginning of the year, but if you do it correctly, it's actually time *gained* over the course of the rest of the year (since you won't have to stop to address minor incidents all the time). I think of this often when working with teachers and teacher leaders in my building, as it relates to delegation.

Implement Documentation Systems

Over the course of several years, I went from being a solo administrator to having an Assistant Principal and a full-time Social

Worker. One particular year I also received a new position of School Counselor, and a full-time Principal Intern. I remember thinking, this is fantastic. I've never had this amount of support before. I'm going to eat dinner at a reasonable hour this year, I'm going to be on top of my inbox again!

Yet I was never busier. Why? Because you can't just delegate things and expect them to be done exactly as you would do them. In reality, I had several new staff members that required coaching, support, and a lot of "I do, we do, you do." I had spent years creating systems for organization and communication and I couldn't just *tell* new building leaders what to do, I had to show them and partner with them enough so that I was confident moving on to the "you do" part. That's when you can truly delegate.

I started to respond to office calls and do building walks in partnership with my newer leaders—school counselor, principal intern, whoever it was on any given year—and as we'd visit classrooms, I'd ask my new leaders what they thought of what we had just witnessed. Whether the feedback was based on instruction, classroom management, or anything at all that they wanted to mention or compliment, it was extremely valuable to hear their thoughts and then share my feedback.

That year, I actually had classroom teachers complaining that students were acting out in class and "nothing was being done." I was initially taken aback—what? We have *seven* people holding walkie talkies, ready to report any time an office call comes in! As I spoke with more teachers, it dawned on me that with so many hands in the pot, things were being missed.

If I reported to Miss Hanson's classroom on Monday because Jasper was flipping his desk and chair over, then I de-escalated him and returned him to class . . . but on Tuesday morning it was my Assistant Principal running there to support because I was in an IEP meeting, then on Tuesday afternoon it was the School Counselor reporting to support Jasper, who de-escalated him and then returned him to class . . . then on Wednesday it was my Psychologist. . . . you get it. If Miss Hanson wasn't writing it up every single time she called the office (and teachers get busy, many forget). . . then it was easy for me to "miss" that this was

Target Team Log 2020–2021						
Student	Grade/HR	Date of initial concern	Concern	Next Steps	Person/People owning next step(s)	Results? Report Out
Name Redacted	4-207	9/17/2020	He is on our radar for having a difficult transition back into school	Check in with wellness team	School Psychologist	Touched base with teacher and student. He reports that he is doing well in school. He does get frustrated with his school work on a rare occasion.
Name Redacted	1-106	9/28/2020	Lethargic, task avoidance, outbursts, defiance, disrespect	504 meeting 10/8, IEP eval note from Dr.	Social Worker	Mother canceled meeting. Classroom teacher reports that she has started a daily motivational chart with student. Teacher and mother share chart via text, daily. Student to begin in-school counseling 11/1.
Name Redacted	4-107	9/28/2020	Frequent elopement	Put Classroom Teacher on team agenda for 10/22	Social Worker	I see student in my first grade group on Fridays. He has permission for break when needed. (He needs to provide a break card)
Name Redacted	5-114	10/5/2020	Impulsive, interrupting, very mobile	Meet with Classroom Teacher, update behavior chart	Psychologist	I provided T with sensory tools, developed break cards. Student utilizing break 2x day. I followed up w/teacher about "appropriate " use of the break card as it was being utilized post poor behavior, which would serve to reinforce the behavior.
Name Redacted	3-202	10/8/2020	Girl friend group- texts/social media in the evenings, which boil over into class	Meet with girls, call/inform parents	Principal	Held productive meetings with students. Reinforced kindness & inclusion. Informed all parents of chat 'drama' and reminded of school social media policy.

Figure 11.1 Example of Target Team Log

happening all day, every day. And teachers were feeling *unsupported* even though we had a record amount of support! Worst of all, the student is not receiving any type of long-lasting support.

We now have a documentation system, and we meet weekly as a Target Team to discuss the office calls and how we responded. Turning around how the school was supporting teachers with students in need of behavioral interventions would require everyone to stay calibrated. This way, teachers weren't facing a revolving door of well-intended staff who respond to the classroom and slap a temporary Band-Aid on a situation, but we were able to work together to dig deeper and work with the child to support identifying the root cause of behaviors and map out a plan for the student to find success.

Every time I respond to a call to support a teacher with a student having a difficult day, I am able to check the Target Team log (in-house, confidential) to ensure that I am up-to-date with steps that have been taken to support this child and his teacher.

Final Thoughts

You cannot do it all. Well you can, but if you try then there is no you left. Knowing what tasks to prioritize, things that *only you* can or should do, and which tasks you can delegate, is key. Delegation is not as easy as assigning a task to someone and walking away. Frequent coaching and check-ins are necessary to be able to truly know that a task is being handled in a way that aligns with your vision, your school goals, and growing and sustaining an excellent culture and climate. Remember to focus on aligning the importance of the task to the quality of the individuals. As you improve the quality of your staff, you increase the number of people important tasks can be delegated to. This allows us to protect the best people and also involve everyone. Best wishes to you and to everyone you delegate to!

12

Building Leadership Inside the Four Walls

As an Assistant Principal, I was so fortunate to have a mentor who modeled so many of the tenets of leadership I hold dear. I was like a sponge; I wanted to impress the principal, I wanted to support the staff, but most of all, I wanted to be as prepared as possible for when I eventually took a principal position at my own school one day.

I never dreamed that I'd be the person who was in the position to develop other leaders as they too began their leadership journeys, but that has been one of my proudest accomplishments as a principal. I hired two Assistant Principals from my own faculty whom I had also mentored as they completed their administrative study programs. They both went on quickly to become principals of their own schools. My third Assistant Principal came to me as a stranger and spent over three years as my partner in turnaround work. She was eager, motivated to learn, and left her own unique mark on the way we do things at our school. All three Assistant Principals affected the journey our school is on in very different ways and further cemented my belief that the goal in hiring is not to put them in line but form a new line entirely.

DOI: 10.4324/9781003321323-17

Developing Instructional Teacher Leaders

When working to turn things around in a school, the owner-ship of every aspect of a school's functioning cannot rest on the principal's shoulders alone. We can develop teacher leaders who can lead from within the structures of a school and who know the school better than any well-meaning district support staff.

At my school, we created a team called the Teacher Laboratory Team that we funded through grant money. Teachers had to apply for a position on the Lab Team. The idea was to support all teachers from within—whether the teacher was struggling, or just hoping to grow in a particular area—pairing them up with an in-house mentor who could coach them on different instruc-tional strategies or ways to implement classroom manage-ment techniques. These Lab Teachers would also open up their classrooms to the whole school, providing opportunities for peer observations. Lastly, these teachers attended outside-of-district professional development to not only enrich their own profes-sional knowledge and practice but to share it with the rest of the school in turn.

The key to these teacher leadership positions—I was very careful to emphasize this—was *not* to call these teachers experts. We didn't want to create an in-house hierarchy between "the people that the principal thinks are the best" and "everyone else." I wanted to promote these positions as brave, courageous teachers who were willing to take risks, willing to open their doors as they themselves were trying new things, and willing to work with a consultant or coach. These positions were promoted first and foremost as opportunities for development and collaboration.

Their first conference was a conference for teachers, by teachers, celebrating teacher leadership: the National Network of State Teachers of the Year Conference. This conference was selected due to its purpose: celebrating teacher leaders, sessions created "for teachers, by teachers," and promoting how to be teacher leaders at your own schools. During the conference, I created a spreadsheet for all teachers to contribute to: they each had a tab and were asked to name each session they attended, what the overarching theme or purpose was, and how they could see this benefitting our school.

The value of attending this conference cannot be overstated. The team came back to school with much learning to share; they created several professional development opportunities which were delivered on Orientation Day, at summer retreats, and after-school. However, the most valuable professional learning opportunities occurred during the school day. Classrooms were opened up for peer observations and Lab Team teachers shared in their process as they implemented new strategies, ideas, and programs. The takeaways from the conference made their way into our school's ecosystem seamlessly.

During in-house professional learning time, our staff members were given choices of a menu of PD sessions in an effort to personalize professional development for all staff. Surveys were distributed so that teachers could provide feedback to each other on the sessions they attended, what they would still like to learn, and what could be improved upon. Most importantly, the practices of the Lab Team now extend across the staff. Lab Team members now recruit other teachers in the building to bring with them to professional learning opportunities, and those teachers now join Lab Team members in creating and facilitating professional development at our school. Several teachers, of their own volition, have presented to the faculty. Empowering a few through the Lab Team initiative became a way to empower all.

I mentioned earlier how important it is to onboard new hires and create a welcoming and supportive environment for all teachers new to our school. The Lab Team became instrumental in doing this, as well. I eventually handed "New Teacher Orientation" over to the Lab Team and asked them to facilitate the sessions based on their areas of expertise. Two teachers would explain our SEL and PBIS initiatives, two teachers went over the special education and Multi-Tiered System of Supports (MTSS) process, and other teachers reviewed our school procedures and routines such as arrival, dismissal, the faculty online handbook, how to request technology support, etc. . . . all the things that veteran teachers don't need to go over as in-depth during the official Orientation Day. I loved seeing our Lab Team take over the responsibility in talking about our school, what makes it such a great place to work, and assuring our new hires that they were there to support them, should they need anything at all.

Developing Committee Leaders

Leading in a school setting is not just about facilitating professional development or becoming an administrator. Leadership can exist in every corner of our building, simply in the way people inspire others to be better and strive for better themselves.

One area of schools that is often in desperate need of teacher leadership is the committees. In my school, I needed to get the right people on board leading the way. We needed in-house leaders who could manage our committees—Parent Engagement, Fundraising, Culture and Climate, Social-Emotional Learning, and even Gardening needed attention! The mere existence of these committees wasn't enough; they needed to be run by committed staff with vision. Far too often, I'd ask one group a question and get jumbled answers—some vision was required.

One of our teachers, Miss Humphries, had a big "end of the year" celebration each June in her classroom for her students and families. She got almost 100% participation year after year. I asked her if she would be willing to take the lead on the Family Engagement Committee and harness her ability to involve parents school-wide. She agreed and recruited several staff members to join her. Our Psychologist took the lead on our SEL Committee, and one of our teachers with a gigantic green thumb naturally took the lead on the Gardening Committee.

All of these buckets of school functioning have the potential to eat up a lot of time. I wanted to be involved with them all but couldn't possibly manage everything. I needed these teachers to not only be the "chairpersons," but be empowered to recruit, motivate, take the lead on initiatives, plan events, and take responsibility for communicating with the staff.

At first, I attended each and every committee meeting. I forgot what my husband looked like. I was constantly at school, morning, evenings, even weekends. I worked with the committee chairs to create a one-pager for each committee that they could use when recruiting members. This included the committee's vision and goals, its role within our school community, the responsibilities of the committee, and the anticipated time commitment for members. We also created a document so that at every committee meeting, a member could take notes on a shared document that is viewable by our entire school. As our school got stronger, so too did our committees. I mentioned the Weekly Bulletin earlier, and how I capitalize on leaders in my building (math coach, Nurse, teacher Lab Team members, and so on) to contribute to the formation of each week's bulletin via a Weekly Roll-up document which captures all pertinent information from their departments. I added my committee chairpersons to the roll-up document, so that they can share upcoming meeting dates, events, and information. There's a set section in each Weekly Bulletin for all our committees to "report out." There is an expectation that the committees are meeting and are sharing updates and opportunities to get involved with our faculty.

The message was clear: our teachers were capable of stepping up and leading in many areas. An outside consultant is not going to come in with all the answers; a district administrator does not have the secret recipe for success—*we* know our building better than anyone. *We* know the needs, from the big-picture to individual classroom needs. *We* were going to turn around the quality of instruction in this school.

My instructional leadership team consists of my Assistant Principal, my reading coach, my math coach, and me. We meet once each week to review data, discuss coaching cycles, and prepare topics for upcoming grade level planning time and professional development. A few times per year we plan for state assessment, or plan special events such as Reading Week or S.T.E.A.M. Night.

Both my current instructional coaches were previously teachers at my school. That has happened a few times over the years; teachers in my school have felt empowered to take on the responsibility of instructional leadership. I love growing leaders in-house for the simple fact that we aren't losing good people who are ready for a change; we get to keep them.

The interesting thing about developing leaders is that by nature, leaders move on. As I worked with Assistant Principals, they move on to eventually lead their own buildings. Instructional coaches have taken jobs at the district level or have made the leap into administration. So developing leaders can be a continuous, cyclical process that starts all over again at a moment's notice. This may seem discouraging, but it also means you are doing an excellent job of recruiting and developing the faculty and staff in your school. You became a leader because you wanted to broaden your impact. Here is another way you are doing so. Thanks and congratulations.

Teacher leaders sometimes decide to take the next step and become instructional coaches to broaden their reach by supporting teachers; yet oftentimes they are very happy doing what they do best—teaching children. What's important to remember is to never ever stand selfishly in the way of a staff member looking to learn, grow, or make change. When my last Assistant Principal told me she was finally ready to take on the role of principal, I simultaneously had two reactions—extremely happy and proud of her, and also devastated for myself because she was so valuable to the smooth functioning of our school and I had been able to confidently delegate many important tasks to her. I knew I would now be starting over, and hopefully be able to find just the right person to take on school turnaround with me. But that's the name of the game. You train them up and then they leave the nest. They, too, will now embark on a journey to make change and shake some branches in a new school. If we've done our jobs correctly, they're ready.

Final Thoughts

A well-known quote from leadership guru Tom Peters is that effective "leaders do not create followers, they create more leaders" (2006). By leading the way for teachers and other staff members to view themselves as leaders, you have the opportunity to expand your influence by expanding informal and formal leaders in your school. And, this multiplier effect continues because then your newly developed leaders have the chance to do the same. This is one of the many things schools work to do. Principals develop people they supervise, and teachers develop students they supervise. When you demonstrate this practice on a schoolwide basis, it allows each of our staff members to learn from your model to give the gift of leadership to students in your school. This is part of the timeless effect as we work to improve our school one person at a time. It is sort of like a pyramid of growth.

13

Sharing Your School's Story

One of the biggest struggles that turnaround schools face is public perception. As I mentioned earlier, for years my school had a well-earned reputation as being "out of control" with "terrible behaviors" and "no structures." Daily substitutes would be assigned to our school for one day and then request that they never be sent back there again. District administrators would feel the negative energy the moment they walked in. Teaching candidates would not apply to our school during yearly hiring fairs.

So how can you celebrate improvements, accomplishments, positive changes in a way that shows the world how much you are growing as a school?

Harness the Power of Social Media

One simple way is social media. Many educators share their school's "highlight reel" on Twitter or other social media outlets. Whether it is Instagram, X (Twitter), Facebook, TikTok, or all of the above, just as leaders created more leaders, social media allows you to brag without bragging. I remember being at a state conference with a colleague of mine, who had a strong Twitter presence. He was constantly tweeting about the positive, wonderful things happening at his school. I would see his tweets and think, "Wow he really has such a fun school, they've got so

DOI: 10.4324/9781003321323-18

many wonderful things happening over there, the teachers look so happy ... Here I am on my third behavior call of the morning, and a teacher just yelled at me because her computer is broken." I said this to him while we were sitting together at the conference and he said, "Of course it looks that way. I'm pretty strategic with what we put out there. Yesterday we had to put a child in a physical restraint; I'm not going to tweet *that*!" This is when it all clicked for me: Of course he had the same issues arise as the rest of us. Of course he had really tough moments. Of course he probably got yelled at some time recently, too. *But we are the filter.*

Some of the second-floor teachers may have heard about the behavioral disruption in fourth grade this afternoon—word always travels. But how many heard about the amazing animal presentations that students did in our third grade? How many of our teachers knew about the Spelling Bee that Mrs. Perry held in our second grade this morning? Did any teachers other than fifth grade know that we had our Safety Patrol pinning ceremony this morning? Most would have no way of even figuring this out. It's so easy to become consumed with what happens within your own four walls and only hear about the negative. *We are the filter.* Not only did I want to share the positive images and successes with the community at large, I wanted the teachers in our own school to see these things, too. I was sharing these photos in our Weekly Bulletin already, but you can't share everything, every week, so social media became an excellent outlet to turn our image around.

For my school community, Twitter quickly became the platform for sharing amongst district personnel, administrator colleagues, teachers in both our school and others, as well as a (inter)national professional learning network. For sharing with parents, Facebook or Instagram was best. Pictures celebrating the conclusion of Reading Week or the Sweetheart Dance got parents involved in our Facebook page practically overnight. Our school has always struggled to increase parent involvement, so even just a bit of social media engagement was more than welcome.

When maintaining a school's social media presence, we can keep four key factors in mind:

1. Consistency
2. Special Guest Stars
3. Branding
4. Uniqueness

1. Consistency

Remain consistent with what is shared and how often. Everyone can share Student of the Month pictures, all-school assemblies, spirit day costumes—and we did. But the things that made us unique, the things that teachers were doing above and beyond the call of duty, we made sure to emphasize. We tweeted from Coffee by the Curb, consistently every Wednesday morning—images of our staff members serving coffee, our parents meeting with teachers and support staff on the sidewalk, our admin team socializing with bus drivers and crossing guards. The tweet wouldn't just be to share the pictures but to convey the information to people reading it that these events were happening, they were now part of our school's fabric, and that they were positive. We shared pictures of our Orientation Day breakout sessions and activities; these pictures depicted teachers bonding, laughing, and working together as a team. We shared pictures of our Walking School Bus initiative, and all the community members who were walking our students to school: fire fighters, public officials, local sports teams. We shared every single ounce of positivity and fun coming from our building.

2. Special Guest Stars

I never passed up the opportunity to invite a "local celebrity" to our school. If we were celebrating Reading Week and had a local news anchor reading to our students, we'd post a picture of it and tweet it out to the district, state, and beyond. If we had city firefighters, we'd memorialize it by capturing a picture. The mayor was stopping by? Snap!

During Reading Week, we try to invite as many Guest Readers as possible so that each room has an exciting guest to look forward to greeting. I'd start early and reach out to every school district member I could: Superintendent, Chief Academic Officer, Director of Operations, everyone! School committee members, other district personnel who may not get out into the schools as much, local politicians, news anchors, athletes, parents, community members—I really mean everyone. We'd always take pictures of the guest readers with our students and share. Spreading the good and focusing on the new culture we were building became a priority.

We didn't just invite people during Reading Week, we invited them to our Back-to-School Bash, to our ribbon-cutting ceremony for our new playground, to every single thing that made sense to open our doors and invite guests to. And this opens the door to begin a relationship with these individuals; it will become a yearly *tradition* to come read at your school, not just a one-time thing.

Local politicians and other notable community members will remember the countless invitations when the time comes that they have opportunities or donations to share. These Special Guest Stars become our extended family and are rooting for the success of our school.

3. Branding

It's common for schools to share using a hashtag to connect the community. Each time we shared a post on social media, we used our school's hashtag. This hashtag united us with a simple message: no longer should we feel like the school no one wants to be a part of or the school the state had neglected for so long. We are *proud* to work here, and *proud* of the work we are doing. We extended the hashtag to our clothing: it's on our staff t-shirts, and I'll use it in captions for our pictures in the bulletin, memos to staff, and messages to families. It has become a part of all of us.

Our mascot is the star. So everything we did—and I mean everything—included stars. Stars on our certificates, stars on our clothing, stars on our murals. We would post pictures on Twitter and instead of calling them students, we'd call our children our stars: check out these stars who just completed their animal presentations!

Teachers caught on and started tweeting with the same hashtag. And we'd tag the district, too, so that the district could in turn re-tweet our posts and "brag" about all the positive things happening in our building. On Orientation Day one year, we created a scavenger hunt for the staff to compete in groups. Every time a group found one of the items, they could earn points by:

♦ Taking a photo of the item they found for 1 point
♦ Taking a photo of the whole group with the item for 2 points
♦ Posting that group photo on Twitter, with our school's hashtag for 5 points

It was a fun competition, and my Assistant Principal and I kept refreshing our Twitter feeds to see the fun photos captured by the group during the 45 minutes we gave them to strategize, go on the hunt, and complete the game. Seeing the smiling pictures of our staff posing with silly hidden objects, tagging the school and using our hashtag, felt great. Anyone from central office or across the district would now see the reality of what was going on at our school: people were happy. The game was also a great opportunity to get more staff signed up for Twitter, and the more people who were "on the bus" spreading the great things that happened at our school, the better.

Curating this sense of pride need not happen only on social media—it can become part of the fabric of your school building itself. We had been gifted a "Day of Service" by a local company who did an annual clean-up day for public organizations such as public schools or city parks. When meeting to plan with their project manager, we had the idea to promote our school pride on a mural right by the front door. It was a huge undertaking, and several volunteers spent the majority of their day on this giant brick wall at our entrance, but it now proudly shows our name in colorful paint with stars incorporated into the design. Every time a staff member, student, or parent walks in that door, they can't miss it! Whether you're reading it consciously or just passing by, it's right there. Welcome to our HOME.

4. Uniqueness

Turnaround is not only about getting the basics right; it's also about going above and beyond in creating an educational environment. Schools have dedicated staff members going above and beyond on their own time, choosing to spend time with students and families after the school day has ended. This is the type of dedication that is worthy of sharing far and wide.

Our school is located in the inner city, with more than half of our population consisting of families speaking languages other than English at home. We also welcome a large Newcomer population: students with limited or no formal education who are new to the country and new to English. Many of our students are from countries with a much warmer climate than New England, so we thought it would be a lot of fun to start an Ice-Skating Club each winter.

The club was a huge experiment for us; we had absolutely no idea what to expect. It was born during the time period where we returned to school after the pandemic shutdown and were slowly returning to our normal routines. Many indoor activities were still prohibited, so we thought of this outdoor experience as a great alternative and a way to continue after-school activities that involved both staff and students.

Our first outing to the large outdoor ice rink in downtown Providence was epic: about 50 students rode the school bus to go skating, and just about every one of them had never put on ice skates before. We were prepared for the amount of support our students would need in finding the right fit with skates, lacing them up, and stepping out onto the ice for the first time. The faculty showed up in large numbers; this was a huge undertaking, and everyone wanted to help. We had children from the Congo, Syria, the Dominican Republic, Afghanistan . . . places where colder climate activities were not as abundant as they are in New England. Watching these students step out onto the ice for the very first time was amazing. Some were terrified, some were fearless, and all had a blast. Some of the adults skated, others stood around the perimeter of the rink to give pep talks to the children who were too nervous to let go of the board—we all experienced something special and exhilarating that day.

We got into a habit of sharing photos of the ice-skating experience on social media, and these pictures naturally stood out amidst all of the classroom photos. They transmitted a single, powerful message: Our school was a family.

Another tradition we started was a "Night Field Trip" once a year to watch a college men's basketball game. The games were usually at 6:30 or 7:00 pm. We handed the tickets out to families but never got a lot of feedback as to anyone attending the game. Some of our families struggle with transportation, and paying for parking around the convention center could be tricky and expensive. My Assistant Principal and I thought, could we get some school buses to take us?

We could, and we did. Students, parents, and staff gathered at the school in the evening, ready to board the bus. We filled one or two buses and headed downtown. Some staff members met us there, but for those of us who rode the bus—what an intimate opportunity to sit and talk to a few families.

Many of our students had never gone to a college basketball game before, and the look of amazement on their faces when they saw the enormity of the arena was exciting to experience. This was an event right in their city, to which they did not have regular access. Parents and students cheered alongside teachers and principals. Our little girls gushed over the cheerleading routines, while fathers were holding up their cell phones recording some of the game. Some of my favorite photos are from those nights, and of course we shared them on social media. How powerful is the image of two of our teachers, sitting on a school bus in the dark of night, speaking with our parents and students?

We were telling our school's story, but more importantly, it was now a story worth sharing. Our school story was no longer just about low test scores we were working to improve. Our school story was students surrounded by dedicated staff, willing to do whatever it takes to get to the next level. Teachers who are invested in our students and who believe in the power of connections. We would continue to work on our instruction, growth, and achievement, but we now had built connections that would lay the foundation for future learning.

Let Others Tell Your Story Too

One of my proudest moments was when my school's story was "told" but not by me, or by a member of the leadership team. It was told by our most valuable players: our students and families.

Each year, the state of Rhode Island conducts a survey called SurveyWorks, which is given to students, families, and school staff to collect critical feedback. Hundreds of thousands of stakeholders participate, to share their feedback or perspective on what's going well, and what needs improvement, in our state's schools.

Some of the topics covered in the teacher survey are: quality of professional development, adequate time to plan for instruction, and satisfaction with school leadership. Students receive questions about school safety, if they feel supported by teachers, and school expectations. Parents are surveyed on how welcome they feel at their child's school, how engaged they are with school events, and how often they meet with teachers to talk about their child's progress.

A few years ago, the annual SurveyWorks results were released, and our school's survey results were at their highest point ever. 82% of responding parents reported that their children enjoy going to school (compared to the state average of 70%), and 76% reported that the lessons at their child's school were motivating (compared to the state average of 56%).

89% of our students answered positively to the question, "How excited would you be to have your teachers again?" and 90% of our students responded favorably to the question "How respectful are your teachers toward you?" 96% of our teachers responded positively to "How respectful are the relationships between students and teachers?" and 93% of teachers responded favorably to "When one of your teaching strategies fails to work for a group of students, how easily can you think of another approach to try?" These responses were surpassing the state and city averages, marking a high point for our school's overall culture and climate.

The Governor and Commissioner of Education took notice. The Commissioner noted at a public meeting that this data was "unprecedented." At a district event hosted at our school, local news reporters were present to capture images of the Governor, who was visiting with our newly-announced Superintendent. I was walking the building with the group, and in between classroom visits, the Commissioner prompted me to share my school's story with the reporters. One asked how we were able to achieve such dramatic change at our school, so I shared some highlights and pride points from our school's story with him, and the other reporters. He asked, "So, what's your secret?" and being caught on the spot (and knowing that he didn't have time to hear all the details of our journey!) I replied, "If I tell you, it's not a secret!" The reporters all laughed and then moved on.

Imagine my surprise when I received a message later that day that the reporter who asked me "what's your secret?" was still interested in finding out. He wanted to do an interview about our school's culture and climate, and how we had made such improvement over the years. When the article was published in *The Boston Globe*, our school was ecstatic. The title read: "This Elementary School Is the Best Kept Secret in Providence" by Dan McGowan.

I sent the following email the morning the article was released:

> *Good morning,*
>
> *Not sure if you have seen the Boston Globe article that was published today about our school, so I wanted to pass it along. I am so proud that our school has been called the best kept secret in Providence . . . you all have worked so hard to turn this school around and we're seeing the change in real time right now. Parents and students are happier than they've ever been. Staff morale and collaboration are at a high.*
>
> *For those of you (you know who you are!) who have been here since the days when. . . .*
>
> - *substitute teachers would complain to Human Resources that they never want to be placed at our school again . . .*

- *the state told you they were shutting our school down . . .*
- *children were running around the school unsupervised . . .*
- *staff absences were so high that you'd have seven or eight students split in classrooms every single day . . .*
- *suspension rates were outrageous . . .*
- *you had three principals in one year . . .*
- *there were holes in the walls, ceilings, and floors. . . . .*

This one's for you.

And for those of you (you also know who you are) who have no idea what that last bullet list is about since you were not here at that time . . . I hope you take pride as well, knowing how much you have contributed to the shift in direction that this school has taken. Thank you for choosing our school, and thank you for making our school a better place for children.

Staff response to that email was heartwarming. It felt so good to see the emails pouring in from staff members who were thrilled our "little school that could" had garnered such positive, widespread attention.

This time, the story of our school was shared in the form of data, collected from our students, parents, and families. It was authentic and personal to the reality of what happens in our building every day, and the climate and culture we were striving so hard to constantly improve. Our school community told the story. And that was due to the hard work of so many.

Final Thoughts

Sharing your school's story is a great way to keep your community informed of the great things that are happening within your building and also, outside of the school day. There are many things to share that illustrate how your faculty and staff are going "above and beyond," so shout them from the rooftops. Not only does it give credit to extremely hardworking people, but it also motivates and inspires others to do the same. Always remember, if you do not share your story, someone else will. Enjoy the opportunity to tell and share all of the wonderful things taking place in your school and in your classrooms. Isn't that part of the reward in all of the hard work? Even if you are hesitant to do it for you, please realize you are doing it as one small, but public, pat on the back for everyone on your team who has worked so hard to make a difference to the young people in your school. Every school has problems. Every school has successes. The more you share your successes they become the core of your school. Make sure the world knows that your school's foundation is a daily array of successes!

Afterword

Are We There Yet?

How do we know when we're there? To be honest, I don't know if any school will ever be *there*. That's the challenge, that's the frustration: there really is no "finish line." Name the perfect school with zero room for improvement. I'll wait.

Our world is evolving and changing. Our student population is rapidly expanding to include students and families from many different backgrounds, and our language learners will always need new scaffolds and supports. Our instructional practices will always need improving. There will always be something! "Turning it around" to me has always held the implication of taking something that has gone off-course and righting the ship. Or taking something that has sunk deep into neglect and giving it the attention, love, and support it needs to thrive again. That said, even the best schools have some things worth turning around.

Pick a Starting Point and Never Give Up

I have one particular "turning it around" story that I think can reach educators in schools of all shapes, sizes, and stages of the improvement journey.

DOI: 10.4324/9781003321323-19

I mentioned earlier when talking about beautifying and improving the physical condition of the school, that I was able to put in a playground. My school had never had one before, so I know that no matter what, a playground is an improvement to the school that mattered to so many people. Our kids and our community deserved a playground! I think about the inequity of even having to write that in a book about turning a school around; so many schools nowadays have big, modern beautiful spaces and structures for children to run and play on. We didn't have *anything*.

Obtaining that playground was an uphill battle the entire way. The city owns the school, not the school department, so everything had to get approval through City Hall, and the red tape was rolled out almost immediately. Then there was the ordering of the equipment and mulch: there were several safety regulations and certifications these items needed before I could get the purchase approved. Then the coordination of the paving, the digging, the installation of the cement structures, the sealcoating company . . . Once we finally got to a place where the playground project was underway, we ran into an unforeseen issue: a sinkhole. I laugh thinking back on that particular day in the hot July heat, as my secretary and I stood around the yellow Caution tape, staring down into that sinkhole, thinking "which class covered this in college?"

I pressed on in the process. I didn't stop until that sinkhole was filled and repaired. Then we had to buddy up with the construction crew. They had been contracted all over the city to complete different tasks, and my playground project was nowhere near the top of their list. Time was ticking away, and school was opening in mere weeks. We were very nervous that we would not achieve our vision of opening school with a brand new playground. My Assistant Principal and I called the contractor and offered to buy him a meatball sandwich—suddenly, we were back on schedule!

By the time that final playground mulch chip had been spread across the playground area, I was emotionally drained. We did it: our school had a playground. I couldn't wait for the children to get back to school and see this. I actually took a mulch chip from the playground that day and pinned it on the bulletin board in my office right under a sign that has the famous quote of the late coach Jim Valvano, "Never, Ever, Ever Give Up."

That's how I've approached school improvement ever since, and it's what I believe will lead to success for anyone looking to turn anything around. Think about that playground story:

- ◆ We identified a need
- ◆ We identified the why: this was important because our children deserved better
- ◆ We reached out for help
- ◆ We had to learn the process and depend on other people
- ◆ We had to coordinate several groups to work toward this vision
- ◆ We ran into an unforeseen complication and had to figure out how to deal with it
- ◆ We pressed on and had to think of creative ways to get what we needed (meatball sandwich!)
- ◆ Most importantly—we never gave up.

You can read through that list with whatever your number one concern is at your school, whichever component(s) of your school that you're hoping to "turn around," and those steps would apply. You've already identified the need—now identify your "why." You'll reach out for help, and you'll need to depend on other people. You can't do this alone; you need to mobilize your groups as you work toward your vision. There will be complications, of course, but don't stop—get creative! Most importantly, never, ever, ever give up. One of the discussions we had was whether to make this book about one school or all schools. We realized that sharing the journey, struggles, and successes of one school allows us to develop a vision and become so determined that we know it can be our school. The journey is the result. Make sure you savor it.

One day, you'll leave knowing you left the school in a better place than how you found it. That is all we can ask of ourselves:

to leave things better and more beautiful, and to know that we've left a positive and lasting impact on our students' lives. You got into education to make a difference. Here's your chance. Enjoy the journey and the destination. They are both something special. Thanks for reading *Turning It Around*. And, thanks for Turning It Around.

References

Peters, Thomas J. and Waterman Jr., Robert. H (2006). *In Search of Excellence: Lessons from America's Best-Run Companies.* Harper Business.

Whitaker, Todd. (2018). *Leading School Change, 2nd Edition: How to Overcome Resistance, Increase Buy-In, and Accomplish Your Goals.* Routledge.

Whitaker, Todd. (2020) *What Great Principals Do Differently, 3rd Edition: Twenty Things That Matter Most.* Routledge.

Whitaker, Todd. (2020). *What Great Teachers Do Differently, 3rd Edition. Nineteen Things That Matter Most.* Routledge.

Wong, Harry K. and Wong, Rosemary T. (2018). *The First Days of School, 5th Edition: How to Be an Effective Teacher.* Harry K. Wong Publications.

For Product Safety Concerns and Information please contact our EU
representative GPSR@taylorandfrancis.com Taylor & Francis Verlag GmbH,
Kaufingerstraße 24, 80331 München, Germany

Printed and bound by CPI Group (UK) Ltd, Croydon, CR0 4YY
08/06/2025
01897003-0012